KING TIGER
VS
IS-2
Operation *Solstice* 1945

DAVID R. HIGGINS

First published in Great Britain in 2011 by Osprey Publishing,
PO Box 883, Oxford, OX1 9PL, UK
PO Box 3985, New York, NY 10185-3985, USA
Email: info@ospreypublishing.com

Osprey Publishing is part of the Osprey Group.

A CIP catalog record for this book is available from the British Library

Print ISBN: 978 1 84908 404 8
Ebook ISBN: 978 1 84908 405 5

Page layout by Ken Vail Graphic Design, Cambridge, UK
Index by Alan Thatcher
Typeset in ITC Conduit and Adobe Garamond
Maps by bounford.com
Originated by PDQ Digital Media Solutions, Suffolk, UK
Printed in China through Asia Pacific Offset Limited

15 16 17 18   13 12 11 10 9 8 7 6 5

The Woodland Trust
Osprey Publishing is supporting the Woodland Trust, the UK's leading
woodland conservation charity, by funding the dedication of trees.

www.ospreypublishing.com

Acknowledgments
I would like to thank the following individuals for their kind support, without
which this book, and my other military history endeavors, might not have been
possible: Charles Lemons, curator, and Brandon Wiegand, asst. curator, Patton
Museum of Cavalry and Armor; Candace Fuller, head librarian, Davis Memorial
Library; Joseph Miranda, editor in chief, *Strategy & Tactics* magazine; Colonel (ret.)
Jerry D. Morelock, PhD, editor in chief, *Armchair General* magazine; Alan
Wakefield, curator, Photograph Archive, Imperial War Museum; Jarosław
Piotrowski; Alex Vasetsky; Stanislav Zharkov; Mikhail Zharkoy; Igor Serdukov;
Mariusz Gajowniczek; John Schaefer; Claude Balmefrezol; and my mom,
Carin Higgins. Any errors or omissions in this work were certainly unintended,
and for these I alone bear responsibility.

Dedication
To my wife, Diana.

Author's note
Army groups, armies, corps, and divisions employ differing
numbering conventions in this book. Some examples are: 1st
Belorussian Front; Eleventh SS Panzer Army (spelled out); XII
Guards Tank Corps (Roman numerals); and 23rd SS Volunteer
Panzergrenadier Division *Nederland* (Arabic numerals). For better
readability German unit names are partially anglicized (e.g. schwere
SS-Panzer-Abteilung 503 is shown as 503rd Heavy SS Panzer
Battalion, "Panzer" being retained as it is commonly known to
mean "armor").

Artist's note
Readers may care to note that the original painting from which
the battlescene color plate in this book was prepared is available
for private sale. All reproduction copyright whatsoever is retained
by the Publishers.

All enquiries should be addressed to:
Peter Dennis, "Fieldhead," The Park, Mansfield,
Nottinghamshire NG18 2AT

The Publishers regret that they can enter into no correspondence
upon this matter.

Key to military symbols

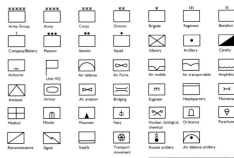

Editor's note
For ease of comparison please refer to the following conversion
table:

1 mile = 1.6km
1lb = 0.45kg
1yd = 0.9m
1ft = 0.3m
1in = 2.54cm/25.4mm
1 gallon (US) = 3.8 liters
1 ton (US) = 0.9 tonnes

Glossary
APCBC/HE-T: Armor-Piercing Capped Ballistic Cap/High
    Explosive – Tracer
HVAP: High Velocity Armor Piercing
APHE-T: Armor-Piercing High Explosive – Tracer
HE: High Explosive
HEAT: High Explosive Antitank

CONTENTS

INTRODUCTION

During the 1920s and 1930s the concept of a heavy "breakthrough" tank was a common theme in European military thinking, when mechanized and armored doctrine was in its post-World War I infancy. Throughout this period, former combatants wrestled with how best to use armor to help avoid repeating the previous war's static and wasteful trench warfare. Soviet futurist military thinkers such as Marshal Mikhail Tukhachevsky envisioned integrated "mobile groups" spearheaded by heavy, multi-turreted T-32s and T-35s that had been organized into independent units. Lighter vehicles, operating much like the Russian cavalry during the Russian Civil War (1917–23), would then be used to quickly push through the breach to initiate "deep battle" missions to disrupt their adversary's command, control, and communications abilities.

Following its proxy participation in the Spanish Civil War (1936–39), leading thinkers in the Red Army refined their views on armor, and while they missed many of the conflict's tactical lessons they excelled in the technical arena. The "mobile fortress" approach with its multitude of guns was seen as flawed and such systems were replaced with single-turreted designs that emphasized simplicity and reliability: assets for the large, undeveloped areas in which such vehicles would operate. Production quantities were also of primary concern and anything that was not absolutely necessary to achieve this goal was suspect. Crew comfort was generally a low priority in Soviet armor thinking, and fatigue and lessened performance was often a problem in the utilitarian working environment.

Throughout World War II armor development and doctrine underwent considerable changes, especially within the accelerated crucible of the Eastern Front. The Soviet T-34/76, introduced during Operation *Barbarossa* in 1941, shocked the Germans with its thick, sloped skin, excellent mobility, and powerful armament.

Although the German heavy Tiger I tank was made operational in August 1942, and could effectively contend with the T-34, the latter's considerable production numbers outpaced the capabilities of the German industry, with the result that the Soviets could better weather a war of attrition. As a result of the rapid arms race in the east where each side attempted to maintain a battlefield edge, vehicle weight, armor protection, and firepower all increased.

After the fighting around Kursk in mid-1943, the Soviets looked to produce a vehicle that had thicker armor to better resist the German high-velocity 88mm gun and a main armament that could handle the armor mounted on the enemy weapon. When the IS-2 ("Iosef Stalin") entered the field in April 1944, its 122mm round imparted considerable force, which helped to make up for its average penetrating ability. In combat it proved well suited for its task as a "heavy" breakthrough tank that could stand up to the German Tiger I and Panther. During the previous month, however, the new German Tiger II had been deployed, and would soon be sent to the Eastern Front.

Although officially designated as "Panzerkampfwagen Tiger Ausf. B," the Tiger II was more often known by its unofficial name, initially coined by the Reich Ministry for Armament and Ammunition, "Königstiger" ("Bengal Tiger"), which was incorrectly translated by Allied intelligence as "King Tiger" or "Royal Tiger." By expanding on the thick armor and large main armament of the Tiger I, and the more modern design of the Panther, the 70-tonne Tiger II presented a formidable battlefield solution. During the final ten months of the war it was as suited to the defensive fighting Germany was forced to undertake as the IS-2 was to spearheading Soviet offensives across Eastern Europe. By 1945 both vehicles represented the epitome of operational heavy tank design that greatly contributed to the postwar, multirole "main battle tank" embodied in, for example, the German Leopard I and II and the T-54/55.

A pristine, two-tone Tiger II with a "series production" (Henschel) turret. It has probably just been produced considering it lacks its bow and cupola armament, spare turret tracks, side skirts, glacis-mounted Bosch headlight, and tow shackles on its drive sprocket guides. (DML)

CHRONOLOGY

1937

January — Henschel is contracted to develop a heavy breakthrough tank that eventually becomes the Tiger I.

1941

June 22 — Operation *Barbarossa* begins; German forces first encounter the Soviet T-34.

1942

September 16 — The Tiger I is first used in combat with 502nd Heavy Panzer Battalion just south of Lake Ladoga, in the Leningrad sector.

1943

February 2 — Krupp's prototype (later "series production") turret is delivered for testing at the Kummersdorf research facility.

July 4–17 — Operation *Zitadelle* takes place in the Kursk area.

July–August — Development of the Tiger II and IS-2 begins.

1944

March 14 — The first Tiger IIs are issued to Panzer Lehr Division's Panzer Company (FKL) 316 as radio-control vehicles for the tracked BIV Sprengstoffträger explosive carrier.

April — IS-2s are first deployed to combat during the Proskurov–Chernovtsy and Uman–Botoshany offensives with 11th and 72nd Guards Heavy Tank Regiments.

July 18 — Operation *Atlantic* in Normandy sees Tiger IIs first used in combat, with 1st Company, 503rd Heavy Panzer Battalion.

August 13 — Tiger IIs are first used on the Eastern Front, at the Sandomierz bridgehead with 501st Heavy Panzer Battalion against IS-2s of 71st Guards Heavy Tank Regiment.

December — The Soviets create Guards heavy tank brigades to organize existing IS-2 regiments.

An IS-2 with a hard-edged welded nose, mistakenly promoted as the first Soviet tank to enter Prague, sits atop a monument in that city's Štefánik Square. Attachments between the towing shackles hold spare track links. Following the "Velvet Revolution" in 1989 the vehicle was painted pink to protest against the former Soviet/Warsaw Pact occupation. (DML)

An early-model "broken-nose" IS-2 that appears to be disabled, judging by its missing return roller and disheveled appearance. Its horn and headlight have remained intact. (DML)

1945

January 12   Tiger IIs from 524th Heavy Panzer Battalion confront IS-2s of 13th Guards Heavy Tank Regiment near Lisów, Poland.
Operation *Konrad* sees IS-2s and Tiger IIs of Heavy Panzer Battalion *Feldherrnhalle* clash during the siege of Budapest.

February 15   11th SS Volunteer Panzergrenadier Division *Nordland* precedes the main *Sonnenwende* operation in an effort to relieve the Arnswalde garrison.

February 16   Operation *Sonnenwende* begins and a corridor to Arnswalde is opened.

February 17   Second Guards Tank Army arrives in the Arnswalde area.

February 21   German forces participating in *Sonnenwende* go over to the defensive as the Arnswalde garrison begins to evacuate.

February 23   With the Germans back to their initial positions along the Ihna River the Soviets renew their general offensive to clear Pomerania.

March 29   The final Tiger II is picked up from the factory.

April–May   IS-2s and Tiger IIs (502nd and 503rd Heavy SS Panzer Battalions) fight against each other for the final time during the Battle of Berlin.

Two IS-2s provide infantry support in Berlin on April 27, 1945. The rough external appearance is apparent on the rear vehicle, which (strangely, considering the location and time) lacks friend-or-foe identification stripes along the turret sides. (DML)

A close-up of a Tiger II of 503rd Heavy Panzer Battalion in Budapest in October 1944, showing the commander's aiming rod, one of the vehicle's three "Pilz" mounts, and the cupola-mounted antiaircraft support, minus its machine gun. Because of the Tiger II's impressive size it was frequently photographed; here it is part of a series of propaganda shots. (DML)

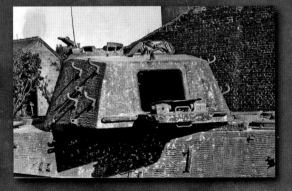

Rear turret view of a Tiger II that is covered in anti-magnetic mine Zimmerit paste and lacks its cupola hatch cover. Because of its weight the rear turret door had a spring hinge to facilitate movement. (DML)

DESIGN AND DEVELOPMENT

THE TIGER II
ORIGINS

By 1942 heavy tank design had advanced considerably since the German manufacturing firm Henschel and Son began development of a 30-tonne *Durchbruchwagen* ("breakthrough vehicle") in 1937. While Germany had been on the strategic offensive between 1939 and 1942, lighter armored vehicles such as the 23-tonne Panzer III (main) and 25-tonne Panzer IV (infantry support) had proved sufficient in the maneuver and exploitation roles. Combat on the Eastern Front, however, necessitated tanks and self-propelled guns of increasing size and firepower as the Germans and Soviets both attempted to maintain an edge in the arms race. As Germany's military stance steadily transitioned to the defensive the continued modification and modernization of existing armored vehicle types would not be a sustainable, long-term solution. An entirely new vehicle design was needed.

Henschel's 57-tonne Tiger I had proved an effective counter to the Soviet T-34, and the heavier KV-1 and British designs, but by mid-war its boxy design was already six years old. The German authorities knew they would eventually need a more modern replacement and Henschel, and their rival Porsche, were subsequently tasked with its development. On May 26, 1942, the German Ordnance Department's Waffenprüfamt 6 (Weapons Proving Office) determined that the replacement for the Tiger I should be able to achieve 40kph, have a main armament capable of penetrating 100mm of rolled

A Tiger II with a production turret (as evidenced by the two-piece barrel), with its Bosch headlight on the glacis and Zimmerit on the hull. The Tiger II was at its best when used as a "sniper," given open terrain and infantry support nearby; the surrounding foliage would provide good concealment for such a position. (DML)

homogeneous armor (RHA) from 1,500m, and possess front and side armor of 150mm and 80mm respectively. Under Waffenprüfamt 6's office head, Oberst Friedrich-Wilhelm Holzhäuer, and chief designer, Heinrich Ernst Kniepkamp, development soon got underway for what would become the heaviest operational tank of the war.

Henschel expanded on their 45-tonne VK (*Vollketten*, "fully tracked") 45.01 (H), essentially a heavier version of the Panzer IV mounting the experimental 75mm/50mm Waffe 0725; this relied on the Gerlich Principle where a skirted round was fired through a tapering barrel to increase velocity, distance, and hitting power. To assist penetration the projectile's tip comprised very hard, dense tungsten-carbide, but as this material was also used to create armor machining tools, limited stockpiles forced the cancellation of the weapon.

Porsche's VK 45.02 (P) proposal was based on their previous attempt to secure the Tiger I contract. The vehicle's weak engine and suspension, high ground pressure, and an over-engineered gasoline/electrical drivetrain – which relied on copper and other materials that would be in short supply for wartime mass production – sealed its fate. Intended to incorporate Rheinmetall-Borsig's new 88mm Flak 41 L/74 antiaircraft gun, it was found to require a breech/counterweight that was too long to fit into turrets designed to house the shorter main armament of the Tiger I. Although Ferdinand Porsche held Hitler's favor, his efforts to produce the Tiger II were canceled on November 3, 1942, in favor of the competition's improved prototype.

As part of this *Tigerprogram*, Henschel's updated VK 45.03 (H) possessed the long 88mm KwK 43 main gun coupled with sloped armor that resembled a bulked-up medium Mark V Panther. To simplify future maintenance and supply, the Tiger II also included transmission, track, engine cooling system, and other components that were interchangeable with the proposed Panther replacement. Hitler's calls for thicker armor and improved maneuverability meant that work on the prototype was slower than anticipated as the vehicle's side panels had to be strengthened during production to compensate for the added weight.

PRODUCTION

Since the 1800s Henschel had been a producer of locomotives, and they were therefore in a position to build a host of combat-related armored vehicles, trucks, aircraft, and artillery in the lead-up to, and during, World War II. Their factory complex at Kassel comprised locomotive and gun production, a foundry, and an armored vehicle assembly works where some 8,000 employees worked in two 12-hour shifts. Instead of an assembly line where skilled laborers assembled components in a sequential manner, Henschel organized production as a series of nine *Taktzeiten* (cycle times), "*Takt*" for short, where large vehicle sections were completed in a defined period before being moved along the line. Bombed some 40 times – often severely, as in a massive RAF raid on October 22/23, 1943 – the company continued to operate in at least a partial capacity until it was overrun by American ground forces on April 4, 1945.

In October 1943, 176 Tiger IIs (including three prototypes) were scheduled to be built at Henschel's factory between November and January 1944. The following month the run of the new tank was expanded by an additional 350, and the order was finally increased to 1,500 vehicles. As Henschel (and Porsche) did not possess the ability to construct the raw turrets and hulls, these were provided by Friedrich Krupp AG (*Aktiengesellschaft*, "corporation"), which along with Dortmund Hörder Hutten Verein (DHHV) and Škoda Works of Czechoslovakia produced main armor components. Turrets would then go to the Kassel-based Wegmann and Company for final assembly before being sent to Henschel for mounting.

As Porsche's design requirement for a 1,900mm turret ring proved too small for the 88mm main armament, Krupp designed one with a 2,000mm diameter to provide a stable platform and accommodate both Porsche's and Henschel's lengthy main armaments with minimal modifications. As Porsche had prematurely created 50 turrets for their VK 45.02 (P) prototype the first Tiger II chassis were so crowned. Externally the "pre-production" turret possessed a curved mantlet (similar to Panther D and A models), which proved resilient, but low impacts could damage the turret ring or deflect a round into the much thinner hull roof. This design shortcoming, and the rather involved construction process, caused the cessation of further such "pre-production" turrets on December 7, 1943. Krupp created the remaining "series production" versions, which featured a *Saukopf* (pig head) mantlet that minimized impact-related jamming of the main gun, and could accommodate many of Porsche's turret components with little or no alteration. Its more simplified armor configuration also resulted in greater internal space so that it held 86 main gun rounds instead of the 80 in Porsche's design.

LAYOUT

The Tiger II's interior and crew positions adhered to conventional German tank layout, with the forward compartment housing the driver and radio operator/bow machine gunner behind the glacis on the left and right, respectively. The driver had an adjustable seat, which could be raised to allow his head to protrude through his open hatch to improve visibility when driving in non-combat environments. Both crewmen had their own hatches and were separated by the vehicle's drivetrain and radio equipment.

The central fighting compartment comprised the turret, which, because of the vehicle's lengthy barrel, needed to be long and roomy to accept the breech's recoil and function as a counterweight. An attached platform/"basket" enabled the turret to rotate as a complete entity with its component parts and floor, which improved safety and operating efficiency. The gunner sat to the left, just ahead of the commander, with the loader to the breech's right. Because of the turret's size it limited the commander's downward visibility from the cupola when "buttoned up." As the Tiger II's transmission and drive wheels were at its front, a universal joint needed to be run under the turret basket to the rear-mounted engine, which increased the vehicle's height by 0.5m, and added to its weight as more armor was needed to cover the difference.

VARIANTS

Although the Tiger II had a 17-month production run few significant changes were made to the basic design. Some vehicles in the first two series (420500 and 420530) had deep fording submersion kits attached, but these were not used outside of testing. In January 1944 flat fenders were replaced with curved ones, straight exhaust pipes were bent to keep exhaust fumes from entering the engine, and a device was added to heat the cooling water to improve starting in wintry conditions. In May, a new type of track was introduced that minimized uneven wear and helped prevent it from climbing over the drive sprocket when in motion. Factory-applied Zimmerit anti-magnetic paste was used on all four series runs until September 9, 1944, when it was mistakenly believed to catch fire following projectile impacts, and was discontinued. Because the vehicle's great weight placed considerable stress on gaskets, seals, and sockets, such components were improved to prevent leaks and breakdowns.

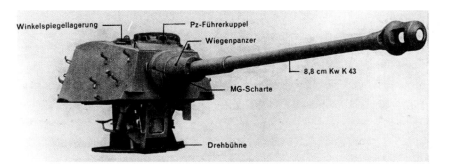

Winkelspiegellagerung — Pz-Führerkuppel — Wiegenpanzer — 8,8 cm Kw K 43 — MG-Scharte — Drehbühne

A Tiger II "series production" turret with its attached basket. Unlike that of the IS-2 this design allowed for the entire fighting compartment to traverse. With greater crew comfort and reduced risk of injuries, the odds of getting the first look/first hit/first kill against enemy armor were improved. (DML)

Tiger II with a "pre-production" (Porsche) turret. The curved mantlet could create a "shot trap" by redirecting incoming rounds down into the more thinly armored upper hull. Appearing fully equipped (minus side skirts and cupola armament), the vehicle is probably en route to operational status. [DML]

Three "Pilz" sockets were welded to the turret's roof to anchor the tripod of a 2-tonne jib crane that was used to help move heavier vehicle components. In July, four track link hangers were mounted to the turret's sides, and retro-fitted to existing vehicles, and in the following month the 20-tonne jack was no longer issued. Starting in November 1944, Wegmann received 20 Tiger IIs for conversion into *Befehlswagen* (command vehicles) housing either an FuG 8 (SdKfz 267) or an FuG 7 radio (SdKfz 268), but these did not re-enter combat until February and March 1945. To prevent rain from obscuring the gunner's view, small shields were fitted over the sight's turret opening, starting in January 1945.

THE IS-2
ORIGINS

When production of the "heavy" KV-1 (named for Marshal Kliment Voroshilov) began in 1939 it was found to have excellent firepower and armored protection when compared to contemporary armored vehicles. Intended as a complement to the more agile "medium" T-34, it was dogged by engine, transmission, and suspension problems. Unable to keep pace in a headlong offensive operation, and often stranded by bridges that could not support its 45-tonne weight, its reliability shortcomings, high production cost, and essentially identical armament to the T-34 made the design increasingly extraneous. A change would be needed, but with the Germans threatening to take Leningrad in the autumn of 1941, the nearby State Plant No. 100 was forced to halt production of the T-34 and KV-1, and join the great industrial migration to relocate in the east. The KV-1's poor combat performance the following year at Kharkov and in the Crimea was the final straw. To avoid the disruption of immediately halting KV-1 production, it was decided to reorganize the vehicles into independent, infantry support tank regiments until a replacement could be produced. By doing this tank brigades would have a more homogeneous composition of T-34s and light armored vehicles.

Once resettled as the Chelyabinsk State Plant No. 100 (ChKZ), the company merged with remnants of related new arrivals such as the Izhora Works No. 187/35, State Plant No. 185 (S. M. Kirov), and State Plant No. 183 (formerly Kharkov Locomotive Works), which specialized in plate armor, heavy armored vehicles, and engines, respectively. To coordinate these armored vehicle production facilities, each was subordinated to the Chelyabinsk Tractor Plant (ChTZ), which had recently transitioned to tank manufacturing. Safely away from the advancing German front lines, and steadily able to overcome quality control issues resulting from the move and integration, the overall organization of seven relocated factories was designated the Chelyabinsk Heavy Machine Plant No. 100 (ChZTM). It was one of the few factories with cranes big enough to lift heavier armored vehicles, and production progressed along a 1km-long main assembly line that was supported by an auxiliary line at designated intervals. To maximize output, workers repeated simple tasks, and all section components remained in one location. Due to the complex's specialized purpose and massive proportions it soon garnered the nickname "Tankograd" ("Tank City").

PRODUCTION

In March 1942 State Plant No. 185's Special Construction Bureau-2 (SKB-2) commenced work on the KV-1's replacement. As with other tank factory design bureaus, ultimate authority rested with the chief designer, Nikolai Shashmurin, who was responsible for day-to-day operations. Under Deputy Chief Zhozef Kotin and his factory chief – who was responsible for meeting production goals – machinists, engineers, and other technicians began work on the KV-13 "universal tank," which was to take on the roles of both the T-34 and KV-1. To minimize weight, while maintaining maneuverability, the turret and much of the hull were to be cast to economize internal space and strengthen key vehicle sections.

A *Landser* from Panzergrenadier Division *Grossdeutschland* inspects a "broken-nose" IS-2, which has suffered a penetration above the driver's position causing an internal explosion and damaging the suspension. The hole in the turret side is a small-arms firing port, minus its plug. Behind vehicle "23" two more IS-2s have also been immobilized; the original photograph may have been altered to make these two appear closer. (DML)

13

TIGER II SPECIFICATIONS

Production run: November 1943–March 1945 (17 months)

Vehicles produced: 492 (inc. three prototypes)

Combat weight: 69.8 tonnes (with "series" turret)

Crew: five (commander, gunner, loader, driver, radio/bow MG operator)

Dimensions

Length (hull / overall): 7.62m / 10.286m

Width (without aprons / with aprons): 3.65m / 3.755m

Height: 3.09m

Ground clearance: 0.5m

Armor (degrees from vertical)

Glacis (upper / lower): 150mm @ 50° / 100mm @ 50°

Hull side (upper / lower): 80mm @ 25°/ 80mm @ 0°

Hull rear: 80mm @ 30°

Hull roof: 40mm @ 90°

Hull bottom (front / rear): 40mm / 25mm @ 90°

Turret face: 180mm @ 10°

Turret mantlet: 150mm (*Saukopf*)

Turret side: 80mm @ 21°

Turret rear: 80mm @ 20°

Turret roof: 40mm @ 78°

Cupola side: 150mm @ 0°

Armament

Main gun: 88mm KwK 43 L/71 (22 turret/64 hull) (typically 50 percent Pzgr 39/43 and 50 percent Sprgr 43)

Sight: *Turmzielfernrohr* 9d articulated monocular (2.5×/5×)

Secondary: 2 × 7.92mm MG 34 (coaxial; bow); additional 7.92mm MG (antiaircraft) (5,850 rounds)

Main gun rate of fire: 5–8rpm

Turret rotation (360°): 10 sec @ 3,000 engine rpm; 19 sec @ 2,000; 77 sec by hand

Communications

Internal: *Bordsprechanlage* B intercom

External: FuG 5 10-watt transmitter/USW receiver (wireless telegraphy and radio telephony stationary ranges were 6km and 4km, respectively; an FuG 2 (USW receiver only) was less common, and had a comparable range)

Motive power

Engine: Maybach HL 230 P30 12-cylinder (water-cooled) 23l (gasoline)

Power/to weight: 600hp (sustained) @ 2,500rpm; 700hp (max.) @ 3,000rpm (10hp/tonne)

Transmission: Maybach OLVAR EG 40 12 16 B; eight forward, four reverse gears

Fuel capacity: 860l in seven tanks

Performance

Ground pressure (hard / soft): 1.03 kg/cm^2 / 0.76kg/cm^2

Maximum speed (road / cross-country): 41.5kph / 20kph

Operational range (road / cross country): 170km/ 120km

Fuel consumption (road / cross country): 5.1l/km / 7.2l/km

Fording: 1.8m

Step climbing: 0.8m

Climbing, degrees: 35°

Trench crossing: 2.5m

10.286m

As the Soviet offensive continued its seemingly inexorable northward advance, by February 3 warmer temperatures and thawing terrain were hampering movement. The commander of one of seven German vehicles that took part in a counterattack to help stabilize the situation southwest of Arnswalde, SS-Untersturmführer Karl Brommann maneuvered his Tiger II near Sammenthin. Although making progress throughout the day, at 0700hrs on February 4 he ran into heavy enemy antitank fire that, when combined with a similar event four days previously, immobilized his vehicle. With Soviet forces threatening to overrun the area three Tiger IIs were brought in to tow Brommann's stricken vehicle back to Arnswalde's central square during the night. From there it was to be withdrawn for servicing.

The Tiger IIs deployed by 503rd Heavy SS Panzer Battalion had been shipped directly from the factory and so Brommann's vehicle would have appeared new, save for any damage from combat or having to maneuver across terrain that could not adequately support its weight. It had a factory-applied "ambush" color scheme, which after early January 1945 was a dark yellow (RAL (Reich Committee for Delivery Terms and Quality Assurance) 7028) basecoat. A hard-edged chocolate brown (RAL 8017) and olive green (RAL 6003) were applied as the vehicle's primary pattern. Small dark yellow (RAL 7028), gray white (RAL 9002), or light gray (RAL 7035) spots were added to the green and brown sections, and olive green to the yellow parts. Internally, the vehicle was painted dark yellow (RAL 7028) as supplies of beige (RAL 1001) dwindled. The turret floor and lower hull were often left in their red oxide primer (RAL 8012), which by war's end encompassed the entire interior as construction times were reduced. Although Brommann's vehicle "221" (the numbers denoting 2nd Panzer Company/2nd Platoon/first vehicle) did not have its number displayed on the turret (unlike the vehicles of 1st Panzer Company, which had them as three black-outlined digits), it did have a Balkan cross. Spare track sections stored on the turret sides acted as additional armor protection. A water-soluble white paint was used to whitewash the vehicles when operating in winter conditions.

The specifications and illustrations are of a Tiger II Ausf B of 2nd Panzer Company, 503rd Heavy SS Panzer Battalion, February 1945 (common to vehicles 269–72, 350–55, and 362–90).

3.09m

3.755m

Rear view of an early model IS-2 with a post-November 1943 rear hull (as evidenced by the engine access ports). Probably immobilized, judging by the surrounding debris, this camouflaged vehicle has its tow cables unhitched and its external fuel and oil tanks are missing. Note the lack of a turret bulge to the cupola's left, indicating a narrow mantlet. (DML)

Within two months a promising prototype was unveiled, but its high speed and horsepower were considerably negated by an underperforming transmission. SKB-2's assistant bureau head (Nikolai Dukhov) and chief designer Shashmurin conducted work on a second replacement design, but the outcome was again mixed. The resulting KV-1S "fast" tank resembled a T-34 turret atop a KV-1 frame, and although it had an improved transmission, numerous structural changes such as weighting armor to the frontal arc at the expense of the rest of the vehicle led to considerable delays.

When the recently fielded, and captured, heavy German Tiger I was evaluated in January 1943, Soviet authorities quickly reevaluated their present heavy tank development program. On February 24 the State Defense Committee (GKO), with General Staff approval, issued decree No. 2943ss ("ss" meaning "completely secret") ordering State Plant Nos 185 (S. M. Kirov) and 100 to develop two new heavy tank prototypes based on the KV-13 that would be capable of dealing with the latest enemy threat. As the 76.2mm L/41 ZiS-5 and 122mm U-11 howitzer were already in production and showed promise against heavier enemy armor, Development Projects "Object 233" and "Object 234" were respectively started.

On September 4, 1943, GKO ordered State Plant No. 100, and its subcontractors UZTM and State Plant No. 200, to improve upon the existing solution. In an effort to distance himself from his disgraced father-in-law, Voroshilov, and gain political favor, Kotin named the new vehicle type "Iosef Stalin." As part of "Bureau IS" (formerly SKB-2), Dukhov favored a design using the KV-13's hull, armor configuration, and suspension, and the T-34's 76.2mm F-34 or the KV-1's ZiS-5. After an unsuccessful attempt to mount a 122mm S-31 main gun into the existing turret, he settled for the smaller-caliber air defense gun M-1939 which was reworked as the D-5T 85mm L/51.6. As with the KV-1S-derived KV-85 ("Object 239"), this IS-85/IS-1 ("Object 237") was also produced in limited numbers from October 1943 to January 1944 as an interim solution. In light of the 85mm gun's sub-par performance against the heavier German Tiger and Panther tanks fielded at Kursk, focus turned to the 122mm U-11 howitzer.

To maintain high production numbers Soviet designers relied on existing gun types as much as possible for their artillery and armored needs. While this simplified production and logistics, the only options for improving a main gun's velocity, accuracy, and penetrative potential were to lengthen its barrel or improve ammunition. Although the 100mm gun outperformed the 122mm A-19 Model 1931 field gun in penetrative capability, weight, and rate of fire, the former was not available in great numbers. By incorporating recoil absorbers and parts from the U-11 howitzer, Kotin's team mated the A-19's barrel to a 122mm howitzer M-30 carriage to produce the D-25T. After successful field testing, "Object 240" was christened the "IS-2" on October 31, 1943, and became operational the following April. To make use of existing IS-1s, Plant No. 100 converted several vehicles to accept the D-25T as "IS-2s," with the remainder being used for training and other non-combat functions.

LAYOUT

With a tank's battlefield life generally brief, the IS-2's designers continued with what had made the T-34 so successful: loose tolerances, simplicity, and ruggedness. Such attributes facilitated mass production and maintenance, and made for a vehicle that could be produced without unduly taxing current manufacturing capabilities. Crew comfort was a secondary concern, and even though the IS-2 had one fewer crewman than the KV-1, the interior was cramped. With only the driver occupying the forward control compartment, the duties of radio/machine-gun operator were taken over by the commander and driver, respectively. To keep from degrading the glacis' integrity and anti-ballistic shape, aside from the driver's vision port, the bow machine gun was rigidly fixed into the hull's forward right side. Electrically fired, the weapon provided little more than suppressive fire along the vehicle's axis. With the tank having only two hatches located in the turret, the driver was in a particularly dangerous position should quick extraction be needed.

The remaining crewmen were stationed in the central fighting compartment with the gunner and commander positioned along the left of the breech and the loader/coaxial

An early-model ChKZ-produced IS-2 near Riga on August 10, 1944. Its D-25T gun has a "German style" muzzle brake (as opposed to the TsAKB style that soon became standard) and a screw-type breech block. (DML)

17

IS-2 SPECIFICATIONS

Production run: April 1944–June 1945 (15 months)
Vehicles produced: 4,392 (+ 107 IS-1s)
Combat weight: 46.08 tonnes (53 percent armor weight)
Crew: four (commander, gunner, loader, driver)

Dimensions
Length (hull / overall): 6.77m / 9.83m
Width: 3.07m
Height: 2.73m
Ground clearance: 470mm

Armor (degrees from vertical)
Glacis (upper / lower): 120mm @ 60° / 120mm @ 30°
Hull side (upper / lower): 90mm @ 15° / 90mm @ 0°
Hull rear (upper / lower): 60mm @ 49° / 60mm @ 41°
Hull roof: 30mm @ 90°
Hull bottom: 20mm @ 90°
Turret mantlet: 100mm (round)
Turret side: 90mm @ 18°
Turret rear: 90mm @ 30°
Turret roof: 30mm @ 85–90°
Cupola (side / top): 90mm @ 0° / 20mm @ 90°

Armament
Main gun: 122mm (121.92mm) Model 1943 D-25T L/43
(28 rounds – typically 20 OF-471/OF-471N (HE) and
8 BR-471 (APHE))
Sight: TSh-17 articulated telescope (4×); MK-IV periscope
Secondary: 3 × 7.62mm DT MGs (2,331 rounds for hull,
coaxial, and turret rear)
Main gun rate of fire: 2–3rpm

Communications
Internal: TPU-4-BisF intercom
External: 10-R; later 10-RK (W/T and R/T stationary
ranges were 24km and 16km, respectively)

Motive power
Engine: 12-cylinder (water cooled) 38.9l (diesel)
(V-2-IS or V-2-K)
Power/to weight: V-2-IS: 600hp @ 2,300rpm
(13hp/tonne) or V-2-K: 520hp @ 2,200rpm
(11.3hp/tonne)
Transmission: Synchromesh (clutch synchronizer),
eight forward, two reverse gears
Fuel capacity: 790l (520l + 3 × 90l external tanks)

Performance
Ground pressure: 0.81 kg/cm²
Maximum speed (road / cross-country): 37kph / 19kph
Operational range (road / cross-country): 150km
(230km with external tanks) / 120km (185km)
Fuel consumption (road / cross-country): 3.5l/km / 4.3l/km
Fording: 1.3m
Step climbing: 1m
Climbing, degrees: 36°
Trench crossing: 2.5m

9.83m

By February 8, 1945, Soviet forces had encircled Arnswalde, and armored spearheads were pushing ahead to reach Kolberg and cut off German defenders around Danzig. North of Reetz Forty-Seventh Army's 70th Guards Heavy Tank Regiment and 397th Rifle Division seemed to have a clear path to achieve this goal as German defenses remained largely fluid. As part of this mix of T-34/85s, trucks, infantry, and artillery, IS-2s were diverted westward to counter a German armor and infantry probe coming out of Ziegenhagen.

After having finished transitioning from KV-1s to IS-2s the previous October many of these crewmen were still getting used to their mounts as they maneuvered through the village of Klein Silber. Although infantry provided small-arms support from the surrounding buildings, a lack of effective communication with the IS-2s resulted in the lead vehicle stumbling into the path of a German Tiger II. Before the Soviet crew could react it was struck between the turret and glacis by an 88mm Pzgr Patr 39/43 and disabled. Anticipating being struck again for good measure those crewmen who could baled out and made their way back to friendly lines.

At this stage of the war the vehicle retained its original green color, over which splattered mud and dust has provided a degree of camouflage. By 1945 Soviet efforts to camouflage armored vehicles beyond their Green "83020 4BO" (basic) security paint jobs steadily declined. For winter, a water-soluble whitewash Type B paint was generally available, and applied by the crew or at the Maintenance Company. As camouflage paint patterns were seldom used, foliage could be substituted. With combat occurring in an increasingly urbanized environment, unit identification became a priority to avoid confusion, and prevent mistaken targeting by friendly ground and air elements. After 1942 this fluctuated among several variations to prevent the enemy from emulating them, such as a white triangle (red during the winter) surrounding a yellow circle. Tactical identification for IS-2 units could be allocated for specific missions by their parent corps or higher commands. IS-2s of 70th Guards Heavy Tank Regiment, like the vehicles of many of the heavy tank regiments, do not appear to have displayed identification numbers on their turrets.

The specifications and illustrations are of a 5th-series IS-2 of 70th Guards Heavy Tank Regiment, February 1945.

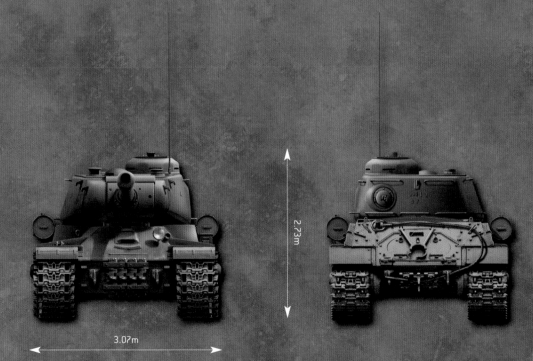

2.73m

3.07m

An early-chassis IS-2 with a partially open driver's visor to help with visibility during operation. A late-war 12.7mm DShK 1938 heavy machine gun is mounted on the cupola of vehicle "35" for antiaircraft use. The splash guard across the glacis minimized the damage caused by small-arms rounds and shrapnel. (DML)

machine-gun operator to the right. Crew efficiency was hampered by the lack of a turret basket, so, to keep the trio from having to negotiate hull components when traversing, each was provided with a suspended seat. As loading the heavy ammunition in such an environment would be difficult, it was stored with the propellant sections in metal, floor-mounted boxes (often covered by a rubber floor mat), while the projectiles were distributed in racks along the turret bustle. F-1 hand grenades and pistol flares were also carried, and the machine guns were mounted for easy removal should the crew be forced to fight outside their vehicle.

The engine and drivetrain took up the rear compartment, which negated having to run a universal joint along the bottom of the vehicle as on the Tiger II. This allowed for a shallower hull that reduced the vehicle's overall height and silhouette. IS-2s had 190- and 245-liter fuel cells in the crew compartment, and one of 85 liters near the motor and transmission. As a reserve, four unconnected 90-liter external cells (three diesel fuel/one oil) were added to the hull's side.

VARIANTS

In February 1944 the Central Scientific Research Institute No. 40 determined that the IS-2's original "stepped" glacis would need 20–30mm of additional armor to effectively resist German 75mm and 88mm armor-piercing rounds. As a solution a single, 60-degree slab of armor provided the required extra strength without an increase in thickness or weight, which necessitated the changing of the driver's plug visor to a simple vision slit. Within four months State Plant No. 200 and UZTM were producing the straightened glacis in, respectively, a cast or welded capacity. Externally welded handrails were also added to assist mounted infantry.

During March a wedge-type breech block was incorporated into the D-25T to facilitate loading, but it did little to improve the system's dismal rate of fire. To vent some of the propellant gas, minimize excessive post-firing smoke caused by poor-quality propellants, and reduce recoil the initial "T"-shaped, single-chamber muzzle brake was temporarily replaced by a more reliable German-style, dual-chamber variety. This, however, restricted vision through the TSh-17 articulated (jointed) telescopic gunsight as it was mounted too close to the breech. State Plant No. 9 in Gorky solved the problem by mounting it further to the left, which meant subsequent turrets had an accommodating bulge beside the cupola and a widened mantlet. The loader's PT4-17 periscopic sight was upgraded to a MK-IV, and a TsAKB (Central Artillery Design Bureau)-designed muzzle brake, which reduced recoil by up to two-thirds, was incorporated as standard. A rear hinge bracket/lock was added to hold the gun in its rear-facing traveling position, and from January 1945, IS-2s were equipped with an external, cupola-mounted 12.7 × 108mm DShK 1938 machine gun for use against ground and air targets.

TECHNICAL
SPECIFICATIONS

THE TIGER II
ARMOR

To resist penetration, tank armor needed to be hard to deflect or shatter an incoming round, but also flexible to diffuse its impact energy and retain structural integrity. Like other heavy, late-war armored vehicles the Tiger II relied on thickness to counter most antitank projectiles of the period. Its hull and turret comprised rolled homogeneous armor (RHA) made from cast ingots infused with chromium and molybdenum to increase deep internal hardening and stress resistance. By compacting and consolidating the metal's microscopic grains to a consistent size and orientation, the plate was strengthened and better able to defeat an incoming round. Homogeneous armor worked best when it was the same hardness throughout, as variations promoted stress concentration boundaries and weakened its ballistic resistance. With the vehicle's glacis and mantlet 150mm and 180mm thick respectively, achieving such consistency was not easy.

As the production process was consistently hampered by Allied bombing, the tempering process of heating the raw metal to 800°C, cooling it in water, re-heating it at a lower temperature, and cooling it again could not always be done to the accuracy required to produce the desired ductility of alloyed steel armor plate. As a result of this "scale effect" a crystalline microstructure (collectively called bainite) could form internally, which increased hardness and the potential for cracking on impact.

TIGER II TURRET

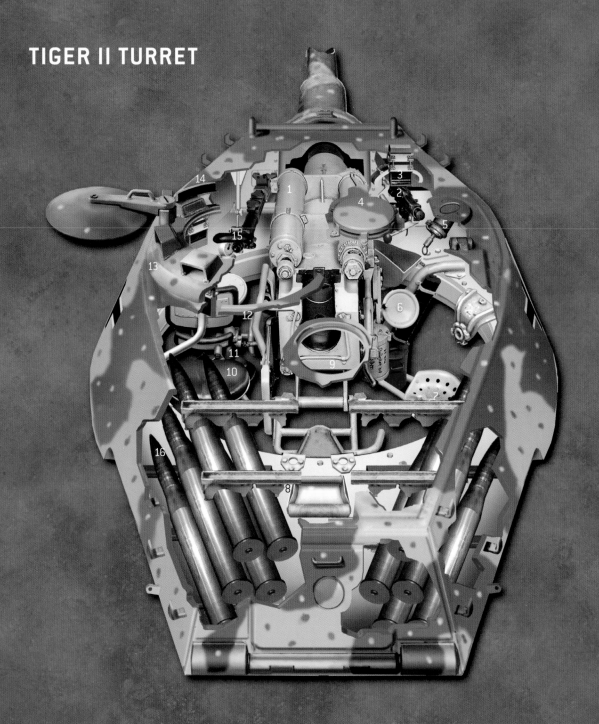

1   Recoil cylinder
2   Coaxial MG 34 (7.92mm)
3   Loader's forward vision port
4   Turret ventilator
5   Localized support port
    (smoke, flares, etc.)
6   Manual turret rotation wheel
7   Loader's seat
8   Ammunition transfer support roller
9   Falling wedge breech
10 Commander's seat
11 Gunner's seat
12 Traverse and elevation wheels
13 Commander's cupola
14 Ring mount for a 7.92mm MG
    (antiaircraft)
15 TZF 9d telescope
16 Ammunition storage

TIGER II AMMUNITION

The Pzgr Patr 39/43 (**1**), an APCBC/HE-T round, was the Tiger II's primary antitank round. Specifically designed to handle the high internal barrel pressures within the KwK 43 L/71 gun, the projectile possessed a tracer and a second driving band for added stability and accuracy over its PzGr 39-1 predecessor (which could still be used provided the main gun had fired fewer than 500 times). Its hard shell was capped by softer metal to minimize disintegration from high-velocity strikes, while the addition of a ballistic cap reduced drag. It also caused armor to crack and weaken before the shell made contact, and promoted better penetration, after which the shell's Amatol (60 percent TNT/40 percent ammonium nitrate) bursting charge would explode. The projectile could also be used by other 88mm guns as indicated by the text on the cartridge, which also gives the weight ("6,900kg"); the explosive charge ("GuRP-G1,5-(725/650-5,1/2"), the manufacturer and manufacture date of the fuze ("dbg1943/1," where "dbg" indicates Dynamit AG); and the manufacturing location and date of the round ("Jg20.1.43K").

The Sprgr Patr 43 (**2**), an HE round, was used against unarmored vehicles, infantry, and static defensive positions. The projectile had no tracer, and except for a second driving band it was the same as the older L/4.7 version. It relied on Amatol explosive; as per the Pzgr Patr 39/43; and the projectile could also be used by other 88mm guns as shown by the text on the cartridge. The text on the shell indicates where and when the fuze was manufactured ("14 Jg20.1.43"); the round's weight class ("III"); explosive ("R8"); and the round's manufacturing location and date ("Jg18.1.43N"). The tip (firing pin and nose) and the piece extending into the round were the AZ 23/28 (*Aufschlagzünder* or "impact fuze"), around which was the main explosive filling. This fuze type could be set for direct-action or delay; it was so sensitive that tank crews were warned against firing through trees or other obstructions just beyond the barrel for fear of premature detonation.

The Gr Patr 39/43 HI (**3**) was a HEAT (high-explosive antitank) that relied on a shaped-charge to penetrate armored vehicles. Again, the projectile could also be used by other 88mm guns as indicated by the text on the cartridge. The text on the shell indicates the kind of round ("HI"); cyclonite/wax explosive ("91"); the fuze manufacturer and date ("Jg20.1.43"); the weight class ("III"), and the round manufacturer and date ("Jg18.1.43N"). The round's tip comprised a small direct-action AZ 38 fuze, which on impact detonated a conventional hollow charge that was set back to allow the conical liner and explosive to properly form a high-velocity metal jet. The rear component is the detonator. As only about 7,000 shaped-charge Gr Patr 39/43 HI rounds were produced their use was uncommon, and the round's low velocity and degraded effectiveness from having to spin made it suspect with many crews.

The Pzgr Patr 40/43 (**4**), an HVAP/-T round, was to be used against the thickest enemy armor. The limited availability of tungsten after 1943 meant that the "HK" (*Hartkernor* "hard core") Pzgr 40/43 armor-piercing composite rigid projectile was also produced with steel ("S" for *Stahlkern*) or iron ("W" for *Weicheisen*) core expedients. The all-black APCR (AKA high-velocity armor-piercing) acted as a kinetic penetrator and had a smaller explosive charge than the Pzgr Patr 39/43. Because of its lighter weight the shell was affected by wind resistance and decreased accuracy. Compared to the production of 1.98 million Pzgr Patr 39/43s and 2.48 million Sprgr Patr 43s, only about 5,800 Pzgr Patr 40/43s were made.

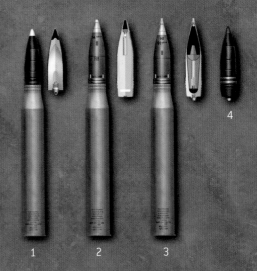

1   2   3   4

Subsequently, an impacting projectile's shockwave would be likely to produce an internal showering of sharp metal flakes known as spall. The Germans tended to use the Brinell scale to determine armor's hardness, which on the Tiger II's glacis and hull sides were BHN 220–265 (150mm) and 275–340 (80mm), respectively. With late-war stockpiles of molybdenum, nickel, and manganese dwindling as the war progressed, vanadium was used as a grain-growth inhibitor to improve the RHA's toughness.

As a smaller profile reduced the chance of being hit, the Tiger II's turret, probably the most exposed part during combat, was tapered in the front, and backed up with 180mm of face armor and a dense, curved "*Saukopf*" mantlet. This meant that when the barrel was pointed at an adversary the turret would either defeat front-on shots owing to that area's great thickness or deflect those striking the sides owing to the great angle. A second benefit of using hard, thick armor was that high-speed incoming rounds often fell into a "shatter gap" where they simply disintegrated on striking the vehicle. Sloped armor also increased the plate's effective thickness. Combined, these aspects translated into the vehicle's frontal armor being essentially impenetrable to existing Allied guns, while side plate armor proved adequate when fighting at the commonly long ranges afforded by the main gun.

ARMAMENT

For the Tiger II Krupp and Rheinmetall-Borsig produced two prototypes of the new 88mm KwK 43 L/71 gun, with the former being an entirely new design and the latter simply a re-worked FlaK 41 L/74. As Krupp's version was shorter, possessed a muzzle brake, and used shorter, more easily stored projectiles it was deemed superior and accepted for production. As an internally mounted variation of the PaK 43 antitank gun it was initially developed with a monoblock barrel and mated to Porsche's "pre-production" turret. Considerable stress from firing high-velocity rounds, however,

A Tiger II hull during the manufacturing process. As part of the "*Takt* 4" process a vertical lathe is being used to machine the opening for the turret. Concurrently, the hull sides would have been prepared for final drive casings. (DML)

necessitated a change to a two-piece weapon, which eased construction and the ability to change barrels. A falling wedge breech block ejected spent shell casings and remained open for another round, and because of the main gun's large size, a muzzle brake was installed both to vent unwanted propellant gases and to reduce recoil.

MOBILITY

To avoid production delays and to maximize vehicle hardware interchangeability, it was decided to use the HL (*Hochleistungsmotor*) 230 P (*Panzermotor*) 30 engine. Built by Maybach, Auto Union (four automobile manufacturers, including Audi), and Daimler-Benz it was being used in other heavy German armored vehicles including the medium 45-tonne Panther and late-model Tiger I. Because of the Tiger II's additional weight a transverse torsion-bar suspension system comprising nine load-carrying axles per side was incorporated. This provided independent wheel movement in the vertical, increased stiffness in turns, helped retain stability over rough terrain, and allowed a theoretical maximum speed of 41.5kph over hard, level surfaces, although a much lower pace was recommended during general operation. As opposed to the Tiger I's interleaved road wheels, its successor incorporated a twin steel-rimmed, rubber-cushioned type, which improved maintenance and cold-weather operation as ice and snow were less likely to impede rotation. Changing gears was surprisingly easy for a front driving sprocket that provided power to the "shoe" and "connector link" style continuous tracks, which were tensioned by a rear idler, and controlled via power steering.

AMMUNITION PENETRATION STATISTICS, 88mm KwK 43 L/71

This table presents the penetration (in mm) of rolled homogeneous armor at 0 degrees and 30 degrees (separated by a forward slash in each case). Although these figures are derived from period Allied and German testing documentation, they cannot be considered completely accurate due to deviations in plate manufacturing and composition, penetration criteria, and ammunition quality.

	100m	500m	1,000m	1,500m	2,000m
Pzgr 39/43 (APCBC-HE-T)	233/202	219/185	204/165	190/148	176/132
10.4kg (warhead), 23.35kg (total); 1,018m/sec					
Pzgr 40/43 (HVAP/-T)	274/237	251/217	223/193	211/170	184/152
7.3kg (warhead); 1,130m/sec					
Gr Patr 39/43 HI (HEAT)	90/90	90/90	n/a	n/a	n/a
7.65kg (warhead), 16kg (total); 600m/sec					

COMMUNICATIONS

Internally, crew communication was conducted through the *Bordsprechanlage* B Intercom. As the standard intercom box installed on vehicles from the Panzer III to

A view of the Tiger II's driver's position showing the two-spoke LSt02 steering device, emergency lateral control lever (to its right), radio racks, and gearbox. To the far right hull ammunition storage is visible. (Author's collection)

AMMUNITION PENETRATION STATISTICS, IS 122mm D-25T L/43

This table presents the penetration (in mm) of rolled homogeneous armor at 0 degrees and 30 degrees (separated by a forward slash in each case). Although these figures are derived from period Allied and German testing documentation, they cannot be considered completely accurate due to deviations in plate manufacturing and composition, penetration criteria, and ammunition quality.

	100m	500m	1,000m	1,500m	2,000m
BR-471 (APHE-T)	Not known/137	152/122	142/115	133/107	118/96
24.97kg; 792m/sec					

the Tiger II, it comprised an audio frequency amplifier for volume control. An FuG 5 ultra-short-wave 10-watt transmitter/USW receiver (Wireless Telegraphy and Radio Telephony) was used for external communication to a range of 6km and 4km, respectively. The associated 2m hollow sheet-steel rod antenna was mounted on a rubber base for additional flexibility when traveling through heavy foliage or under low obstructions such as bridges.

A view of the Tiger II's commander and gunner positions next to the turret traverse wheel. The device mounted to the turret ring is an azimuth indicator displaying 1 to 12 o'clock. Note the metal attachment on the gunner's seat for the commander's foot to rest upon. (Author's collection)

IS-2
ARMOR

In an effort to increase production numbers and keep costs low by avoiding complex, expensive milling facilities the IS-2 incorporated cast armor as much as possible. In contrast to the extensive machining used to construct the German Tiger II, casting involved little more than producing a mold into which molten metal was poured and allowed to cool. The process gave the flexibility to make armor of various thicknesses and curves, and by virtue of the latter exposed less exterior surface area for the equivalent volume, but it also produced several inherent imperfections.

Externally, cavities (risers) needed to be incorporated into the mold to compensate for a metal's quality of shrinking and becoming denser as it cooled, and the areas where the molten metal entered the cast (gate marks) needed to be removed once the armor had cooled. Unlike RHA the grain structure was not rolled or otherwise modified, and was therefore not as strong or resilient. Because of contemporary manufacturing technologies

A Tiger II crewman inspects the front drive sprocket under the driver's position. As no access panel or suspension component is in the area, debris probably needs to be removed. (DML)

and techniques, Soviet cast armor suffered from inconsistent thicknesses across the same mold. To accommodate for such differences turret and hull tolerances were kept loose and minor fitting modifications were occasionally needed.

Internal flaws due to improper heat treatment or the use of low-quality alloys were also common, which with the substitution of manganese for nickel resulted in a hard, high-carbon finished product, especially along the weld seams. Soviet armor plate averaged BNH 420, which on the IS-2 was an even more brittle BNH 450 and BNH 440 on the turret and hull respectively. In general cast armor was hard and resisted penetration better than steel, but it was also more prone to shattering. Although higher-quality Lend/Lease US steel was becoming more available, an attempt was made to harden the armor using tempering in order to better defeat uncapped armor-piercing rounds, but it was abandoned owing to increased production times and cost.

ARMAMENT

As the D-25T was essentially the M1931 A-19 field gun, the IS-2's main gun initially incorporated the same interrupted screw-type breech block and a recoil system consisting of a hydraulic recoil buffer and hydropneumatic recuperator, both located inside the cradle under the barrel. While well suited for attacking infantry and defensive positions, the IS-2's large bore fired a shell with considerable mass that could buckle or deform even the strongest enemy armor should penetration not result. Although the vehicle's BR-471 antitank round traveled at just 77 percent of the Tiger II's Pzgr 39/43, it produced 1.45 times more muzzle energy.

Unlike the Germans, with their variety of antiarmor projectile choices, the Soviets relied on just the armor-piercing, high-explosive (APHE) round, of which the IS-2 carried eight. Soviet armor-piercing projectiles improved after late 1943 as their steel

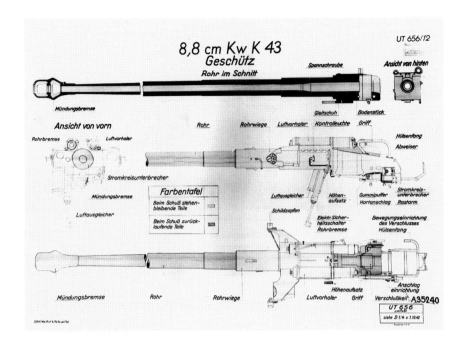

increased in hardness from 460 BHN steel to 550, each increase of 10 BHN roughly equating to a 1 percent improvement in penetration. A more advanced BR-471B armor-piercing capped round (APHEBC) that was better able to penetrate sloped armor was ordered in the spring of 1945, but arrived too late to be issued for combat in Europe. The IS-2's remaining 20 rounds were blast/fragmentation (HE) OF-471 or OF-471N rounds, which gives an idea of the kinds of targets the vehicle was most likely to encounter.

MOBILITY

As developing a new engine for the IS series was not possible due to time constraints and cost, Kotin simply upgraded the one being used on the KV-1. To ensure that the vehicle started in very cold temperatures the IS-2 had a manual and electric capability, with a backup relying on compressed air. A high-pressure NK pump worked with an RNA governor to regulate fuel flow and engine speed as well as preheat the fighting compartment. A multistage air cleaner was also added as the loose tolerances on Soviet armored vehicles resulted in a considerable amount of debris in the oil. The mechanical,

A D-25T with its mantlet, breech block, and TsAKB style muzzle brake. [DML]

IS-2 TURRET

1	D-25T elevation gear	7	Turret elevating gear	13	MK-IV periscope
2	Gunner's seat	8	D-25T breech	14	Turret traverse motor
3	Spare MG ammunition drums	9	Interrupted screw breech block	15	DT coaxial machine gun
4	Manual turret rotation mechanism	10	D-25T securing bracket for travel	16	Loader's seat
5	Turret intercom panel	11	Ventilator	17	Commander's cupola
6	TSh-17 telescope	12	BR-471 APHE-T shells		

IS-2 AMMUNITION

1   BR-471 (APHE-T)   2   OF-471N (HE)   3   OF-471 (HE)

The armor-piercing 122mm BR-471 ("БР-471" in Cyrillic), a base-detonating ("МД-8") APHE-T round (1), comprised an RDX-based explosive ("А-IX-2") and tracer to assist in penetration and targeting visibility, respectively. The red band on the cartridge indicates that it should be paired with the BR-471. The shell's deep grooves helped control its breakup during impact and maintain the explosive charge's integrity until detonation. From top to bottom, the text on the cartridge reads: "ПОД БРОНЕБ" (under armor), "Ж-471" (charge-471), "122-31/37" (referring to the 122mm A-19 field gun, which was also known as the M1931/37), "122-СУ И ТАНК" (for SU-122 assault gun or tank use), "НДТ-3 19/1 1/45N" (charge mark), and "2-45-02" (the date of production).

The OF-471N ("ОФ-471Н") short HE round (2) used Amatol ("АТФ-40") (60 percent TNT/40 percent ammonium nitrate) as an explosive, while the OF-471 ("ОФ-471") long HE round (3) used Trotyl (indicated by "T") (70 percent tetryl/30 percent TNT); "ОФ" indicates fragmentation high explosive. Both of these semi-fixed rounds incorporated an RGM (point detonating) fuze and could be used against armored and static defensive targets alike. When used against armor the large-diameter round produced an effect resembling a squash head where the powerful explosive produced shock waves and spalling. Except for the text on the charge indicating a normalized (H) steel shell ("ЖН-471") the text on the cartridge is identical to that shown on the Ж-471 used for the BR-471.

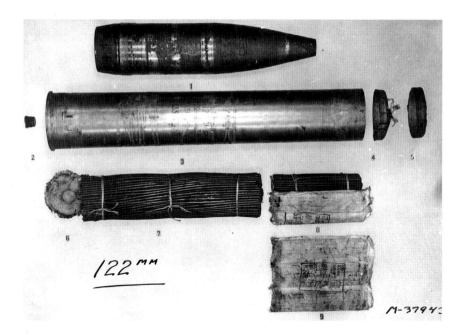

A 122mm OF-471 HE shell and the internal components of its cartridge. (DML)

detachable transmission made for easier maintenance and used a multiple dry main clutch, mechanical gearbox with a reduction gear, and a planetary two-step traversing gear. Although the Christie suspension proved a successful design on the T-34 it did not function well with vehicles over 35 tonnes. As such the IS-2 incorporated a German-derived torsion bar system with all-steel wheels encompassed by lighter "Chelyabinsk tracks" that featured alternating flat links, and excellent traction.

COMMUNICATIONS

For internal communication IS-2 crews used a TPU-4 telephone/intercom system incorporating headphones within a crash helmet and an uncomfortable, rugged throat microphone. Early vehicles were fitted with the same 10-R simplex (unidirectional) lamp heterodyne short-wave radio as had been used in the T-34/76 from the beginning of the war. It operated between 3.75 and 6MHz with a voice range of up to 24km when the vehicle was stationary (16km when moving), with non-vocal communication such as Morse code used as an alternative. As was common, the device comprised a separate transmitter and receiver, each with a rotary transformer, which were mounted on a rubber-bushed shock pad. Most IS-2s contained an improved, more easily produced 10-RK radio, which offered the same ranges, and allowed for the smooth selection of operating frequencies, often with an accompanying 4m umbrella antenna.

THE STRATEGIC SITUATION

GERMANY ON THE STRATEGIC DEFENSIVE

Following the encirclement and destruction of Axis forces at Stalingrad, Soviet forces spent the next two years conducting an inexorable strategic advance that recaptured all of their lost territory, and continued beyond their pre-1939 borders into Eastern Europe. Supplied with substantial Lend/Lease logistical assets, especially badly needed transport, the Red Army were frequently able to concentrate overwhelming numbers of men and machines at sectors and times of their choosing. Their effective use of *maskiróvka* ("deceptive measures") and a growing level of operational experience meant that the Germans were often forced to react to an unexpected or unfavorable situation. With Soviet forces seemingly in strength everywhere along the front German command and control could not consistently or effectively prioritize and address threats and their combat formations were frequently forced to withdraw or risk destruction.

During the summer of 1944 this scenario occurred on a grand scale where the Soviet *Bagration* offensive virtually annihilated Army Group Center. Hitler's belief that the Red Army would try to use their recent acquisition of the western Ukraine as a springboard from which to attack into Romania, Hungary, and southern Poland prompted him to reposition much of his armor south to contest such a move. Instead, the Soviets launched a devastating offensive further north that drove a massive wedge into Belorussia. Unable to regain their strategic balance following Stalingrad and Kursk, the Ostheer ("East Army") traded space for time, while they tried to re-establish adequate defenses and solidify the front. To compound their difficulties, Hitler continually interfered with the war's conduct and the actions of experienced commanders on the spot. By acting as both Supreme Commander and head of the OKH (Army High Command, in charge of the Eastern Front), his authority was unencumbered by other opinions, with predictably disastrous battlefield results. Had the German General Staff been employed as the primary military decision-making entity for which it was established, such a desperate situation might well have been avoided.

THE LOSS OF POLAND

Hitler, continuing to rely heavily on intuition, believed that the Soviets' next great offensive would be against his East Prussian and Hungarian flanks. The head of Fremde Heere Ost (Foreign Armies – East), Generalmajor Reinhard Gehlen, disagreed. His position within Army Intelligence overwhelmingly indicated that the Red Army would instead attempt to capture Berlin and much of central Europe before the western Allies were in a position to contest it. This seemingly indisputable evidence on Red Army dispositions and intentions was passed to Army Chief of Staff Generaloberst Heinz Guderian, and then to Hitler who promptly refuted the assessment. Although outwardly Hitler expressed his belief that the battlefield situation was a Soviet ruse, in fact the Führer's longstanding dislike of Gehlen's direct manner and pessimistic view of Germany's present ability to offer effective resistance meant the findings were not acted upon. As a consequence, Marshal Georgy Zhukov's 1st Belorussian and Marshal Ivan Konev's 1st Ukrainian Fronts were able to capitalize on their achievement against far less opposition than would have otherwise been possible. In mid-January 1945 the pair were able to quickly overrun Poland and establish several small bridgeheads across the Oder River from near Stargard to south of Breslau.

To help stem the flood of Soviet forces moving across Poland, Guderian proposed the creation of an emergency army group to bolster the much weakened Army Group Center (soon renamed Army Group North). On January 24, Hitler gave his approval, but instead of an experienced commander, he assigned Reichsführer-SS Heinrich Himmler to the task, proclaiming that his long-time henchman's exceptional skills at administration and motivation would soon stabilize the situation. In addition to being the head of all branches of the Schutzstaffel (SS), including the Waffen-SS, Himmler had also been put in charge of the Replacement Army following the attempted July 20, 1944 assassination of Hitler by members of the Army. In principle this gave him discretion over where to allocate such manpower resources, often for political rather than military reasons. Himmler's recent performance as commander of Upper Rhine High Command, an independent theater-level formation

A crewman working with a "broken-nose," narrow-mantlet IS-2's muzzle-brake cover. Such protection would be used in transport to keep dust and debris from entering the barrel. Note the female soldier atop the turret. (DML)

answering directly to Hitler, and its ill-conceived operation against French and US forces around Colmar instilled little confidence in the experienced senior officers who were aware of the impending operation.

In preparation for the counterattack from east of Stargard German reinforcements were soon moving through Stettin to create the new Army Group Weichsel (Vistula). Among these, III (Germanic) SS Panzer Corps was steadily pulled from the isolated front on the Courland Peninsula (Latvia), organized at the Hammerstein Training Area southwest of Danzig, and sent to Himmler to act as his command's linchpin. Instead of deploying his forces across the most direct route to Berlin, however, the Reichsführer-SS arrayed the various subordinated replacement and recently separated units in parallel to the Baltic coast in an effort to defend the whole of Pomerania. Zhukov, confident in his superiority of 3:1 in infantry and 5:1 in armor and artillery, simply ignored what he believed to be a "phantom" force, and continued to focus westward toward the German capital.

As Konev approached the Oder, Zhukov's forces encircled the city of Posen on January 24. As Posen was a major transportation hub, the resulting German defense presented a considerable disruption to Soviet logistics between Warsaw and Berlin. As with other Hitler-designated *Festungen* (fortresses) the city was expected to be held at all costs, in part to draw large numbers of the enemy into static, attritional battles that favored the defender. To encourage German efforts to defend the homeland to

An operational view of the fighting in Pomerania following the Soviet Vistula–Oder Offensive, January 28–February 15, 1945.

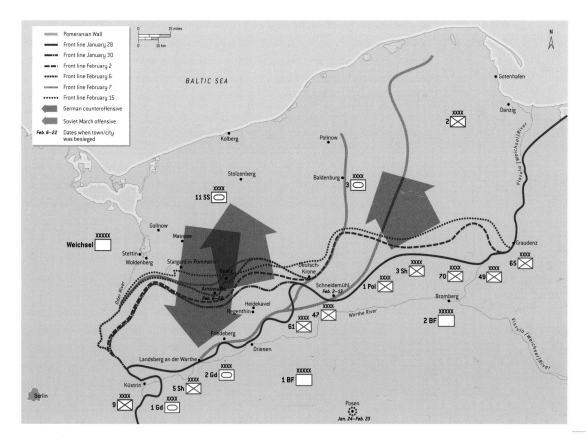

Overturned T-34 Model 1941s that were probably caught by artillery or an air-to-ground attack. What looks to be the explosion's by-product is now a water-filled shell hole. (DML)

the fullest, civilians were often ordered to remain in forward areas at risk of being overrun. As soldiers fought for these "live" cities, all knew the dangers of surrendering to the Red Army, with its widespread list of atrocities against not only Germans, but Poles, Hungarians, freed POWs, and others. Compounding the atmosphere of terror, fever-pitch propaganda spewed from both sides calling for a fight to the death, while behind the German lines Feldjägerkorps, overzealous Hitler Youth, and other groups roamed the rear areas to summarily execute anyone not carrying official documentation granting them permission to be away from the combat zone.

On January 27 lead Soviet armored units crossed the Draga River at Neuwedell, and appeared to herald the imminent collapse of the Pomeranian front. German forces erected makeshift barricades at important crossroads, and scrambled to establish defensive positions with ad hoc, predominantly infantry forces possessing few heavy weapons. Even supply and "non-essential" personnel were thrust into front-line duty, which did little except further disrupt German logistics. Others assisted the flood of westward-fleeing refugees attempting to stay ahead of the advancing Soviets, and reach relative safety beyond the Oder and Elbe rivers. Public officials, motivated to save lives, often permitted populated areas to be evacuated, against orders from the regional Gauleiter or higher authorities. As the front line receded toward towns like Arnswalde, Reetz, and Stettin residents tried to help the passing refugees, but sandwiches and coffee were small comfort to those who had recently lost everything save what could be carried personally or transported on carts. Trucks and trains that were available removed what civilians they could, but as the latter had to burn on low-quality coal substitutes such as lignite their operating effectiveness was reduced by as much as 60 percent. When the Red Army cut the direct routes between Deutsch Krone and Stargard on February 4, such operations through the Arnswalde area largely ceased.

A T-34 Model 1941/42 being shelled by artillery. (NARA)

HALT AT THE ODER

Much as had happened to the western Allies following their breakout from Normandy, the speed and magnitude of the Vistula–Oder operation had placed a considerable strain on Soviet logistics. Second Guards Tank Army, for example, started out from the Vistula with 838 tanks and self-propelled guns. After advancing an average of 40km per day, when Colonel-General Semyon Bogdanov's command reached the Oder in early February its infantry and armor forces were reduced by a third. Unlike the Germans the Soviets were increasingly well supplied as production and transportation services substantially grew during the last half of 1944. Guns larger than 76mm, heavy armor, and aircraft production were a priority, but getting these resources to where they were needed was another matter, especially ammunition and petrol, oil, and lubricants (POL). As the withdrawing Germans practiced a scorched earth policy of destroying and denying as much as possible to the pursuing Soviets, the latter needed to create infrastructures from scratch as they advanced.

With German defenses presently disorganized and undermanned, Soviet commanders deliberated on whether to press immediately for Berlin or to wait for their supply chain to catch up. The latter would allow the enemy time to solidify their own position. On the other hand, to push immediately beyond the Oder invited disaster as Zhukov's First and Second Guards Tank Army spearheads would be vulnerable to encirclement; similar events, such as the failure of the Red Army's headlong advance after Stalingrad, which was pinched off and shattered by Generalfeldmarschall Erich von Manstein, or the sudden defeat of Russian forces at Warsaw in 1920, seemed to justify these concerns.

On January 26 and 27, Zhukov and Konev respectively submitted plans to the Stavka (Soviet High Command) for the encirclement of the German capital. Zhukov proposed to take Berlin in a *coup de main* beginning around February 1, while his peer favored pushing past Breslau to act as a southern pincer in which both fronts would surround the German capital. With Stalin siding with Konev's option, Soviet forces were hurriedly reorganized in preparation for offensive action west of the Oder River slated for between February 4 and 8, with Berlin's capture to follow on the 15th. In the interim Zhukov determined that the Germans would make a stand along the Schwedt–Stargard–Neustettin line to defend Stettin and the Pomeranian coast, while additional forces would probably deploy east of Berlin to defend the direct route to the city. To address these perceived eventualities he sent Fifth Shock, Eighth Guards, Sixty-Ninth and Thirty-Third Armies west to secure bridgeheads over the Oder. The remaining First Polish, Forty-Seventh, Sixty-First, and Second Guards Tank Armies were positioned along the Falkenburg–Stargard–Altdamm–Oder River line to cover Zhukov's northern flank.

General der Panzertruppen Heinz Guderian, commander of XIX Corps, in France in 1940 (note his officer's sword pommel). His chief of staff, Oberst Walter Nehring, follows; his Iron Cross clasp, indicating that he earned the award during World War I, is attached to the chest ribbon. (DML)

Lieutenant-Colonel Peter Mzhachih, commander of the 88th Guards Heavy Tank Regiment, near Küstrin in early spring 1945. His awards include the Orders of the Red Star, Great Patriotic War (both classes), and Red Banner. (Courtesy Mikhail Zharkoy)

Neither Sixty-First Army's advance toward Arnswalde nor Rokossovsky's combat-depleted 2nd Belorussian Front before Danzig was able to advance quickly due to enemy resistance. This resulted in a 100km gap between the two groups, which Zhukov moved to plug. On February 1 Zhukov issued Order No. 00214, which disengaged Second Guards Tank Army from combat along the Oder in order to rest, replenish, and form a northward-facing reserve between Landsberg and Schneidemühl. Other Soviet armored units between Küstrin and the Neisse River were similarly trading positions with infantry, so as to be fresh when they would once again spearhead the coming Soviet ground offensive against Berlin.

By early February the very cold winter weather of the previous several weeks had given way to intermittently warmer temperatures. Although sleet and freezing rain remained the resulting thaw hampered movement and the Red Army's ability to establish forward air bases from which to support the ground forces. The Oder River had correspondingly flooded to a width of up to 6km, and although the Soviets possessed the resources to effect crossings the added prospect of strong German resistance made it inadvisable at present. On February 5, Sixty-First Army struggled to plug the gap on Zhukov's right as a general lack of fuel meant that what was available was allocated to combat and staff vehicles only. When Konev broke out of his Oder bridgehead three days later, the Germans needed to present an effective response, as ever-smaller territory was available in which to withdraw.

GERMAN PREPARATIONS

With all the military setbacks Germany had suffered over the last two years, their increasingly short supply lines, and effective resource management by Albert Speer and others, permitted their rapid reaction to the faltering Eastern Front. Between January 20 and February 12 the Kriegsmarine (German Navy) and hundreds of transport ships, as part of Operation *Hannibal*, had evacuated some 374,000 refugees and thousands of wounded soldiers from sectors cornered against the Baltic Sea and threatened with annihilation. Salvaged combat formations were redirected to Pomerania's defense to contest what was believed to be an impending thrust by Second Guards Tank Army to capture the area around Kolberg on the Baltic coast. Should the German Second Army become isolated from the rest of Army Group Weichsel, the Soviets would unhinge German efforts to protect the province and split east toward Danzig and west for Stettin.

In early February, Guderian looked for a way to pinch off the Soviet spearheads that had advanced to the Oder River before follow-on forces could strengthen the positions. The German bridgehead at Küstrin, and Sixth SS Panzer Army further south, presented resources to launch the right hook coinciding with a similar attack from around Stargard. Should such a limited two-pronged counterattack linking up around Landsberg prove successful, Zhukov's westward advance would be temporarily stymied,

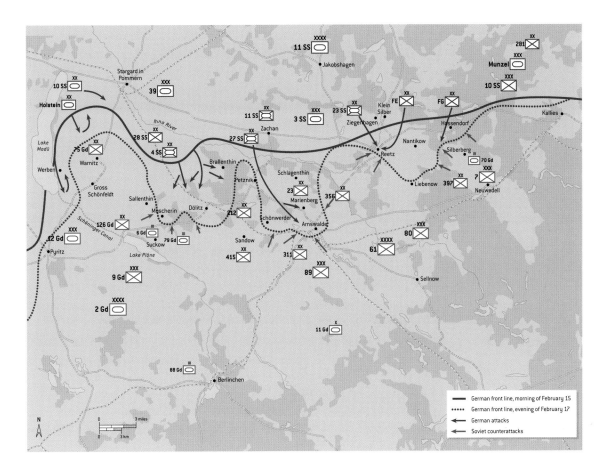

A tactical view of the start of Operation *Sonnenwende* showing two days of German progress following their jump-off on February 15, and the areas of Soviet resistance.

and the resulting time could be used to strengthen Berlin's defenses and possibly to secure an armistice. As additional forces would be needed for such an endeavor, Guderian lobbied for the reallocation of formations from sectors he felt no longer contributed to the war effort, such as at Courland, Italy, Norway, and the Balkans, to what should have been the primary endeavor to protect Berlin. The Führer, however, would have none of it. Sixth SS Panzer Army, recently released from fighting in the Ardennes on the Western Front, had been sent to Hungary to try to retain the region's oil facilities. With hopes for a two-pronged operation quashed, Guderian settled on assembling the remaining northern force to attempt a more modest operation.

While German ground forces adjusted to new positions along the Oder and Neisse rivers the Luftwaffe was responding similarly. The Air Fleet in charge of the area, Luftflotte 6, had expanded from 364 aircraft on January 6 to some 1,838 fighters, bombers, transports, and reconnaissance planes by February 3. Overflights east of the Oder had also increased, with 2,409 on February 1, 1,805 on the 2nd, and 1,995 on the 3rd, as had air-to-ground action. Although Guderian hoped his strongest asset would be surprise, Zhukov did not need his VNOS (aerial reconnaissance, warning, and communication service) to know that the increase in enemy air traffic indicated that a German counterattack was in the offing. Unsure of the time and direction, he continued to reposition his forces and prepared for such an event as best he could.

OPERATION *SONNENWENDE*

Considering the chaotic German military situation in 1945, Guderian was able to assemble a surprisingly large force consisting of three and a half divisions from Third Panzer Army (recently evacuated from near Königsberg) and two re-formed Panzer divisions. In accordance with Hitler's order that this gathering force was to be entirely Waffen-SS, SS-Obergruppenführer Felix Steiner was put in charge of the hastily organized, corps-sized Eleventh SS Panzer Army. As a former select member of the prewar Reichswehr, and an experienced battlefield commander of such multinational forces as 5th SS Panzergrenadier Division *Wiking,* Steiner seemed to be the natural selection for such a daring, late-war endeavor.

On February 8, Stalin abruptly canceled the impending offensive against Berlin, and instead ordered that Rokossovsky's 2nd Belorussian Front first clear Pomerania. Although logistical problems and encircled enemy "fortresses" presented temporary problems, Stalin was motivated by political considerations as well. The western Allies had been held west of the Roer River and the Westwall (Siegfried Line to the Allies) for the last six weeks as Hitler's long-sought-after counteroffensive in the Ardennes ran its inevitable course. Eisenhower's forces were only now renewing their eastward drive into Germany and would not come near those territories that Stalin coveted, but did not yet control, for some time.

After eight days of stockpiling food, fuel, and ammunition for Guderian's counterattack, by February 10 less than half of the estimated requirements had been obtained. With the attack scheduled for the 22nd, Third Panzer Army were not likely to arrive in time to participate. Eleventh SS Panzer Army, with their subordinate XXXIX Panzer, III (Germanic) SS Panzer, and X SS Corps, would be all that was available for carrying out the overly optimistic mission of fighting through the Soviet Sixty-First Army and advancing on to the Küstrin–Landsberg area to cut off Second Guards Tank Army spearheads. Even as Steiner's force accumulated reinforcements, many had to be quickly returned to combat to prevent Soviet penetrations of the front line and preserve his assembly positions.

During a conference with Hitler on February 13, Guderian proposed that as Rokossovsky's 2nd Belorussian Front was now threatening to cut off Danzig, Eleventh SS Panzer Army needed to go over to the offensive in two days to divert Soviet attention and resources. Hitler and Himmler were reluctant to start such an operation until sufficient supplies were gathered, but Guderian managed to secure approval for an amended start date. To gain a measure of operational control, and provide the greatest chance for success, he had his young – but very skilled and experienced – protégé, Generalleutnant Walther Wenck, allocated to command the operation, which was codenamed *Husarenritt* ("Hussar ride"), later changed to *Sonnenwende* ("Solstice").

THE COMBATANTS

THE GERMANS

When the 57-tonne Tiger I tank first entered German service on the Eastern Front in August 1942, it was made even more formidable as an individual battlefield weapon by being grouped into independent heavy armor battalions of up to 45 vehicles. Originally intended to add an offensive, heavy-combat element during German breakthroughs, after mid-1943 these formations were increasingly used in defensive "fire brigade" or mobile reserve roles to help shore up threatened sectors. With exceptions made for research, training, and allocation as company-sized complements to select Army and Waffen-SS divisions, Tiger I and II units were subordinated to corps and army-level commands. Throughout the war, ten heavy Panzer battalions were created for the Army, which operated in North Africa, Italy, northwest Europe, and the Eastern Front. After April 1943 four more were to be organized for the Waffen-SS, with three coming to fruition as 101st, 102nd, and 103rd Heavy SS Panzer Battalions serving under I, II, and III (Germanic) SS Panzer Corps, respectively.

Initially, heavy Panzer battalions officially comprised 20 Tiger Is and 16 Panzer IIIs that were organized into two armored companies, each of four platoons; two of each vehicle were allocated per platoon, plus a Tiger I for each company commander, and a pair for battalion command. As Tiger I and II production increased, the "medium" vehicles were eliminated from the roster. On November 1, 1944, the heavy Panzer battalion received its final company TO&E (KStN) designations: 1107 (fG) (Staff); 1176 (fG) (Armor); 1151b (fG) (Supply); and 1187b (Maintenance).

Recruiting posters in German-occupied areas sought to promote the idea of a unified European effort to resist Communist Russia. Historical figures or cultural elements were often used to tie the present struggle to some noble past endeavor.
(Public domain)

TRAINING

As with the German Army, Waffen-SS inductees first went through several months of intensive infantry basic training; this was so rigorous that in the early part of the war one-third did not finish. Physical fitness, small-arms skill, and political indoctrination were especially stressed. Upon completion of initial instruction individuals could apply for specialized training, for example as officer candidates or engineers, or for service in the armor branch. For the role of tanker those with mechanical or technical skills

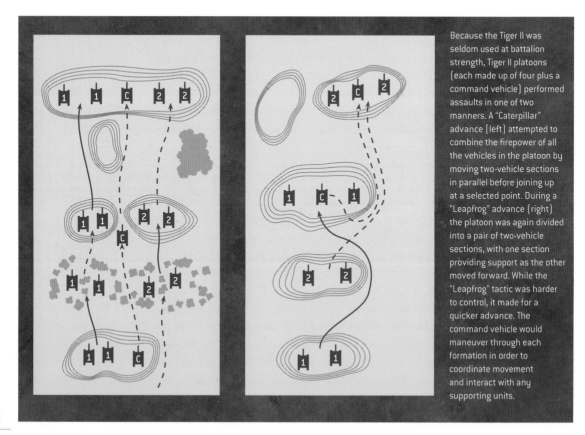

Because the Tiger II was seldom used at battalion strength, Tiger II platoons (each made up of four plus a command vehicle) performed assaults in one of two manners. A "Caterpillar" advance (left) attempted to combine the firepower of all the vehicles in the platoon by moving two-vehicle sections in parallel before joining up at a selected point. During a "Leapfrog" advance (right) the platoon was again divided into a pair of two-vehicle sections, with one section providing support as the other moved forward. While the "Leapfrog" tactic was harder to control, it made for a quicker advance. The command vehicle would maneuver through each formation in order to coordinate movement and interact with any supporting units.

ORDER OF BATTLE, 503rd HEAVY SS PANZER BATTALION, JANUARY 29, 1945

Actual armor strengths are underlined as xx; TO&E/KStN values for armor and manpower are not

Commander: SS-Sturmbannführer Friedrich (Fritz)
  Herzig
Total strength: 45/39 (832 men)
Staff & Staff Company (171 men)
Group Leader: 3/1
Reconnaissance, Engineer, Antiaircraft Platoons
1st Panzer Company: 14/13 (87 men)
Group Leader: 2/1 (17 men)
1st, 2nd, 3rd Platoons: 4 each (60 men in total)
Change crew (10 men)
2nd Panzer Company: 14/13 (87 men)
Company HQ: 2/1 (17 men)
1st, 2nd, 3rd Platoons: 4 each (60 men in total)
Change crew (10 men)

3rd Panzer Company: 14/12 (87 men)
Company HQ: 2/1 (17 men)
1st, 2nd Platoons: 4 each, 3rd Platoon: 3
  (55 men in total)
Change crew (10 men)
Supply Company (258 men)
Group Leader, Damage Clearance and Repair
  Services
Medical, Fuel, Munitions, Administration Sections
Workshop Company (142 men)
Group Leader, Workshop, Recovery Group, Armory,
  Signal Equipment Workshop, Spare Parts Group,
  Supply Train

were naturally most in demand, with training conducted at one of several armor facilities throughout the Reich. Although each crewman was to become familiar with each other's duties, the need for strong interaction among the commander, loader, and gunner was particularly stressed, as close cooperation among this trio translated into rapid responses to battlefield threats.

Because officer candidates and enlisted personnel trained together the sense of comradeship between the two groups was correspondingly strengthened. Where the Army instilled a distinct separation between officers and the lower ranks, the Waffen-SS promoted mutual respect, and a more relaxed atmosphere in which officers were simply addressed by their rank without the traditional "*Herr*" prefix. After 1943 foreign volunteers (preferably Nordic, but also non-Germanic) joined in increasing numbers, in part to fight against what was seen as a Communist threat against European civilization. Although Hitler desired to incorporate these elements into the whole to instill the concept of a united "Germania," Swedes, Norwegians, Dutch, French, and others were organized according to nationality.

Tiger II crews focused on achieving surprise and executing decisions quickly. Once fields of fire were established, terrain was to be exploited for protection and concealment. Enemy armor and antitank guns were priority targets, and against overwhelming numbers the tankers were to scatter and regroup to a more advantageous position. On spotting hostile tanks, the Tiger II was to halt and get ready to engage them by surprise, estimating the enemy's reaction before launching an attack. The crew should hold fire as long as possible, and, if possible, the enemy tanks should not be engaged by a single tank so as to apply maximum firepower.

As Germany's manpower pool, resources, and leverage to achieve any sense of a negotiated peace dwindled, 503rd Heavy SS Panzer Battalion, like other armored formations, was increasingly forced to train on obsolete foreign and domestic tanks. More modern vehicles such as the Tiger I were needed at the front and the battalion's complement correspondingly dwindled. The *Tigerfibel* (the Tiger I manual, which was also applicable to the Tiger II), defined several guidelines for the vehicle's official operation and deployment within a heavy armor battalion. In practice, however, deviations were unavoidable, and at the commander's discretion. To facilitate these, emphasis was laid on the importance of rapid communications between the battalion and its parent command, as such formations required as much time as possible in which to get organized and allocated to a threatened sector. There was also a heavy reliance on armored engineers to strengthen bridges and clear minefields ahead of the heavy tanks.

TACTICS

Panzerwaffe doctrine stressed offensive almost to the exclusion of defensive combat, as evidenced by the 1941 Army Service Regulation *Heeres-Dienstvorschrift* 470/7 (regarding medium Panzer companies), and similar Army Regulations. At most the latter was considered applicable for ambush and a position from which to counterattack. Armor regiments and battalions were doctrinally to employ one of three offensive actions. Firstly, in a *Vorbut* (meeting engagement), an advance force, generally at least company-sized, was employed for taking an enemy by surprise so as to gain key terrain or a similar objective. Alternatively, *Sofortangriffe* (quick attacks), often conducted using the *Breitkeil* (broad wedge) formation (a reverse wedge with two platoons forward and the remaining platoon providing flank support as required) were used when supporting forces were not readily available and immediate action was needed. Finally, an *Angriff nach Vorbereitung* (deliberate attack) could be conducted as a complete unit against prepared defenses.

As a result of the German Army's effective training and discipline, commanders were generally given a considerable degree of flexibility in carrying out tactical and small unit operations. Given little more than the mission and the leader's intention, commanders could conduct an operation, while adjusting to battlefield situations as they occurred. This was perhaps best exemplified in the Panzerwaffe where timely intelligence, security, march discipline, and communications were especially important elements in achieving victory on the battlefield.

When the Tiger I made its combat debut in November 1942 its battlefield tactics and the operations of heavy armor battalions were largely improvised by the crewmen based on their personal experiences. By the time the Tiger II was first fielded in early 1944, a more established doctrine had been developed to address specific battlefield eventualities in a unified manner. Officially, four-vehicle armor platoons were to deploy in either a *Linie* (line) (section leader/vehicle/platoon leader), a *Reihe* (row) (platoon leader/vehicle followed by section leader/vehicle), a *Doppelreihe* (double row), or a *Keil* (wedge), but in practice terrain, the situation, and the commander's experience meant these "parade" formations were seldom used.

503rd HEAVY SS PANZER BATTALION

On April 15, 1943, III (Germanic) SS Panzer Corps was formed to organize 5th SS Panzergrenadier Division *Wiking* and 11th SS Volunteer Panzergrenadier Division *Nordland*. Ten weeks later *Nordland*'s 11th SS Panzer Regiment (two battalions) completed Tiger I training at Grafenwöhr (southwest of Berlin), and for the next three months it served in an infantry capacity, taking part in its corps' anti-partisan operations in Croatia and in the disarming of Italian forces following Italy's surrender in September. On November 1, 1943, II Battalion, 11th SS Panzer Regiment, was re-designated 103rd Heavy SS Panzer Battalion, and was soon sent to the training grounds at Wezep in the Netherlands, and later to Paderborn in northwest Germany. Just prior to the Normandy invasion in mid-1944 the battalion was ordered to transfer its trained crews to 101st and 102nd Heavy SS Panzer Battalions as they would soon be fighting in the region. For the next few months the men of 103rd Heavy SS Panzer Battalion (re-designated 503rd Heavy SS Panzer Battalion on November 14, 1944) trained a new batch of crews, which after October 19, 1944, were allocated Tiger IIs.

THE SOVIETS

Like other nations, during the 1930s the Soviets attempted to find the most effective organizational balance for their light, medium, and heavy tanks. Cooperation with the German Reichswehr, and combat experience gained at Khalkin Gol and Poland (1939), Finland (1939–40), and elsewhere, led to a reconsideration of fielding large mixed corps formations comprised of a variety of tank types and weights. They were simply too large and awkward for most of their commanders to control effectively, and unnecessarily taxed logistics. To address the inconsistency of vehicle types, the well-balanced and maneuverable T-34s were organized as homogeneous tank brigades. The heavily armed and armored "breakthrough" tanks such as the KV-1 were hamstrung by weight and mechanical unreliability, and could not keep pace with their medium brethren. Consequently, these vehicles were structured as independent, direct infantry support tank regiments.

In February 1944 the Red Army began re-equipping their heavy tank regiments with IS-2s and giving such units the designation of "Guards," which was based on such units' weapons and role, rather than any outstanding previous performance. The KV-1s, KV-85s, and British Lend/Lease Churchills were phased out, being outdated and generally unsuited for breakthrough roles, and having suffered high losses in combat. Where the T-34 was to retain its role of exploiting offensive penetrations by

A US Army collection point showcasing a variety of weapons including an IS-2 barrel and mantlet (with damage around the TSh-17 telescope's viewport), and BR-471 antitank round. The table displays a pair of two-piece US M20 3.5in rocket launchers ("Super Bazookas"), several 88mm guns, and what looks to be a 37mm FlaK 43 antiaircraft gun. (DML)

Majors from 88th Guards Heavy Tank Regiment stand with their commanding officer (Mzhachih, third from left) near Küstrin in early spring 1945. The IS-2 pictured was one of only two that remained following heavy losses incurred since starting from the Vistula River. Note the *shapka-ushanka* lambswool hats. (Courtesy Mikhail Zharkoy)

quickly moving into the enemy's flanks and rear, as per Soviet deep penetration doctrine, the IS-2 units were to create the initial opening in enemy lines. In this capacity, they were to capture and hold key locations such as road intersections and river crossings until larger forces moved up, at which time they would either continue to the next objective or return to reserve status for any maintenance, etc.

Of the war's 123 named Guards heavy tank regiments, 58 possessed IS-2s. The remainder retained different heavy tanks such as the KV-1, were disbanded, or were reconstituted. Nine Guards heavy tank brigades were subsequently re-fitted with IS-2 regiments. In practice the component regiments were often sent into action separately, and paired with self-propelled guns that moved alongside infantry to subdue stubborn enemy defenses.

TRAINING

During the initial period of the Russo-German War the Red Army had suffered catastrophic materiel and personnel losses, a problem compounded by Stalin's prewar purges of some 43,000 members of the officer corps. New formations had to be created without the guidance of adequately experienced armor commanders, and this resulted in an incomplete and all-too-brief training regimen. As the commanders who remained feared failure as a consequence of deviating from established doctrine, creativity and initiative were replaced with an inflexible adherence to orders and institutionally optimal solutions to battlefield situations. This rigid approach to training, while often aiding rapid combat responses by junior officers, proved ineffective when encountering unforeseen situations.

Where the two-man turrets of the T-34 and KV-1 forced the commander to double as loader, the IS-2 had enough internal space for a more effective trio. The "Iosef Stalin" was assigned two officers (commander and driver), and two sergeants (gunner and loader/mechanic). Because of the dangerous missions these heavy tank forces would undertake, the additional officer was seen as a way to provide command redundancy, and lessen the chances of the crew shirking from their assigned duties.

COLONEL BORIS ROMANOVICH EREMEEV

Boris Eremeev was born to a peasant family on December 23, 1903, in the western Ukrainian village of Mykhalkove. At age 21 he graduated from the Uman Vocational and Technical School and applied his training toward agriculture before being drafted into the Red Army in 1925. Three years later Eremeev graduated from the Frunze Military Academy, essentially a staff college/graduate school, and joined the Communist Party as an official prerequisite for his new command rank and position.

During the Great Patriotic War Major Eremeev initially served as Chief of Staff for 33rd Tank Regiment. Following the German summer offensive in 1942, he was made Chief of Staff for XVIII Tank Corps between July 7 and September 20, 1942, north of Stalingrad, and during the city's encirclement three months later. As a slightly weaker equivalent to a contemporary German armor division, the tank corps' mix of engineer, motorized infantry, antiaircraft, and roughly 150 KV-1s, T-34s, and T-70s translated into a nimble, all-arms formation that was better able to weather combat than its 1941 predecessors. On February 22, 1943, Eremeev was promoted to command XVIII Tank Corps' 107th Tank Brigade, which was nearly destroyed during Manstein's counteroffensive.

During Operation *Citadel*, Eremeev served as Chief of Staff for XXX "Urals Volunteer" Tank Corps between March 18 and September 21, 1943. He then commanded 244th Tank Brigade *Chelyabinsk* until October 23, 1943, and for another four months after it was converted into 63rd Guards Tank Brigade *Chelyabinsk*. On March 28, 1944, Eremeev was given command of 11th Guards Heavy Tank Brigade, a post he would hold until one day after the official end of the war in Europe in 1945. Eremeev went on to win the Order of the Red Banner for helping to eliminate German defences at Kovno, and later the Order of Lenin. On May 31, 1945, he was presented the Gold Star Medal of

Boris Romanovich Eremeev, commander of 11th Guards Heavy Tank Brigade. A colonel at the time of *Sonnenwende*, he is shown here with his postwar rank of major general of tank troops. Above the various commemorative and campaign decorations hangs the Gold Star Medal of the Hero of the Soviet Union. [Courtesy Igor Serdukov]

the Hero of the Soviet Union for his efforts during the Battle of Berlin. Made a Major General of Tank Troops six weeks later, Eremeev graduated from the Higher Academic Courses of the General Staff Military Academy in 1948, and served for the next nine years until his retirement. He died in Kiev on March 21, 1995.

IS-2 officers, having passed through one of the country's tank academies at Ulyanovsk, Saratov, Gorky, and elsewhere, would train on the IS-2 either with 1st Guards Tank or at the Chelyabinsk or Salikamsk Tank Academies. Starting in May 1943, this year-long course (often just eight months) produced second lieutenants. Higher regimental and brigade officers could attend the J. V. Stalin Academy of the WPRA Mechanization and Motorization Program, which, along with promotion, brought increasing privileges as part of the officer corps.

NCOs received roughly three months of training that comprised specialized class work and training on the IS-2, focusing on loading, aiming, and firing the main gun, ammunition care, radio operation, and technical and mechanical skills. At Chelyabinsk 30th and 33rd Tank Regiments had been allocated for applying tactical procedures, negotiating a variety of natural and constructed terrain types and obstructions, and, about a third of the time, performing night maneuvers, as well as undergoing driver training (all too short). Most of the cadets possessed little, if any, armored combat experience. For the final stage of training, crews were sent to 7th Training Armored Brigade at Chelyabinsk for regimental and brigade instruction, where following the usual send-off fanfare acknowledging the responsible factory workers, newly produced IS-2s were allocated to their new owners.

TACTICS

Soviet armored tactics were inspired by actions such as the 1916 Brusilov Offensive during World War I (1914–18), and later the Russian Civil War (1917–21) and Russo-Polish War (1919–20). Many of the early senior armor commanders such as Uborevich, Triandafillov, and Tukhachevsky had led cavalry forces during these periods, and were correspondingly responsible for developing much of the Red Army's mechanized and armored "deep battle" doctrine. During the 1920s "Black" Reichswehr officers, looking to circumvent the restrictive Versailles Treaty, which forbade Germany to possess tanks, cooperated with their Soviet contemporaries by carrying out covert armored company- and battalion-sized maneuvers. In return for technical and tactical knowledge, German commanders such as Guderian received hands-on experience at the secret training facilities near the tank factory at Kazan known as Panzertruppenschule *Kama*.

Although Soviet armored battlefield tactics steadily improved after 1942 as commanders gained experience, they continued to opt for the simplest battlefield solutions that promoted fighting spirit, and stressing ultimate victory over efficiency and initiative. By the end of 1943, however, Soviet tank and mechanized formations had matured to a point where new organizational structures were not created. Instead, existing formations were improved by the incorporation of specialized forces, which, based on Stavka's determination, resulted in armored formations being more flexible and balanced than previous mixed structures, thus fitting better within the Soviet technical and tactical capabilities. An insufficiency of radio sets remained a command and control problem, and limited communication between higher commands and their subordinate units, as well as with close air support.

While the Germans used combined-arms battlegroups (*Kampfgruppen*) to undertake tactical goals, the Soviets applied a similar approach with the *peredovoi otriad* (forward detachment). These mixed formations generally consisted of a tank brigade that was supported by infantry and self-propelled guns, which operated up to 100km in front of the main Red Army force to exploit weaknesses in the enemy's lines. Up to two days before being committed to battle, participating Soviet armored forces assembled 10–15km behind the front line. Supporting formations such as infantry, engineers, and artillery would also arrive on the scene where they would be task-organized to a depth of 1.5–2km. On the night preceding action, armor and support units would move up to within 1–3km of the forward edge of battle to take up their final positions along an area roughly 1km wide and 2km deep. Generally, a Soviet artillery barrage heralded an offensive, as it tried to soften enemy defenses before a ground assault, especially along the axis of advance. Preceding a Soviet armored breakthrough, sappers (engineers), worked in groups of twos or threes to clear paths through landmines or other obstructions, while aircraft, infantry, and armor attempted to neutralize enemy antitank positions.

During a breakthrough attempt the lead battalion-sized group kept 40–50m intervals between vehicles in the lead, while 200–300m behind, the motorized infantry battalion provided a mix of specialized units such as mortars, antitank, engineer, and assault infantry. Additional heavy armored brigades or regiments (and assault guns) would provide support, as would T-34s on the flanks. Without dedicated armored personnel carriers, the subordinated motorized submachine-gun battalion would ride into battle using Lend/Lease jeeps or simply on the tanks. Around 12 of these *desant* personnel (tank-riding infantry who dismounted to fight) could be transported on an IS-2 until about 1km from the forward edge of battle, when they would dismount and attempt to provide infantry support for the armor. This made it difficult to exploit

IS-2s of 79th Guards Heavy Tank Regiment with welded hulls. Note the horn and extended main-gun travel lock on the nearest and farthest vehicles, respectively. (Courtesy Mikhail Zharkoy)

49

When assaulting enemy positions IS-2 regiments employed tactics that relied on varying numbers of medium T-34/85s and motorized (mounted) infantry making the initial attack (1) and thereby softening enemy defenses and uncovering points of weakness or heavy resistance. IS-2 heavy tanks and ISU-152 self-propelled guns followed in a second echelon, between 300m and 500m behind. This second-echelon force would concentrate on heavily defended enemy positions at ranges of up to about 1,500m, where their large-caliber rounds proved very effective against area targets. With T-34/85s and artillery covering the flanks (2), the heavy Soviet armor would then move forward to lead the immediate breakthrough phase (3). After disrupting enemy command and control and containing any counterattacks the armor would spearhead any pursuit or exploitation.

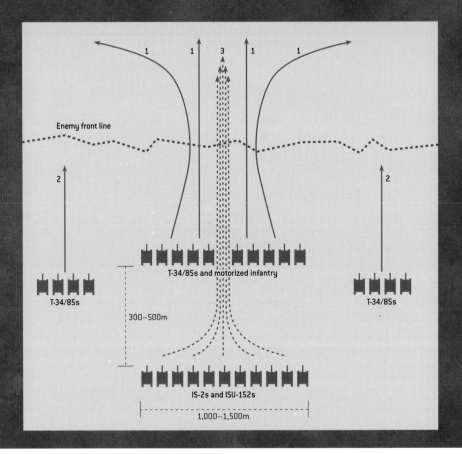

a successful breach as to remain integrated the tanks or self-propelled guns needed to advance at the pace of their accompanying infantry.

Once a breakthrough was achieved, self-propelled artillery was brought forward to help neutralize the area and keep enemy reinforcements from intervening. Firing while on the move resulted in such inaccuracy for any main gun of the period, even those with stabilizing mechanisms, as to make hitting anything other than an area target all but impossible. IS-2 crews (like other Red Army tankmen) relied on the proven fire-and-movement techniques that enabled one vehicle to advance while covered by a stationary partner, and then switch roles after a certain distance.

In defense, IS-2 regiments and their self-propelled artillery support could form a mutually supportive checkerboard formation along the expected enemy path, as well as a mobile reserve. In an urban environment, traditionally the most dangerous for armored vehicles, commanders attempted to get IS-2 formations beyond these potentially built-up areas as soon as possible in an effort to retain momentum, and keep the enemy off balance and unable to develop effective defenses. "Fortress" cities such as Posen and Schneidemühl were simply bypassed, and reduced by predominantly infantry forces.

While IS-2s at least possessed a radio receiver, only company-level commanders and above had transmitters as well. This was seen as an efficient means of inter-vehicle communication as it cut down on cross-chatter and promoted the top-down command style favored by Soviet leadership. During combat, commands were generally made in the open in view of the narrow time frame in which they would be carried out. Specific unit and commander names were coded to preserve security. In addition to radios signal flares were used, as were telephones for more stationary facilities, and although the latter were susceptible to being cut by artillery, they provided the most secure method of communication. Commanders were expected to be at the fore of their tactical commands to provide timely control.

11th GUARDS HEAVY TANK BRIGADE

11th Guards Heavy Tank Brigade had been formed from the nearly destroyed 133rd Tank Brigade on December 8, 1942, as per NKO order No. 381. Two months later the brigade became operational and was assigned to Second Guards Tank Army, which was forming in the Stavka's Strategic Reserve. In August 1944 it was transferred to 1st Belorussian Front as an independent formation along the Warsaw sector, and by year's end it traded in its KV-1s for IS-2s by incorporating 90th, 91st, and 92nd Heavy Tank Regiments, which had recently formed in the Moscow Military District. Throughout its existence 11th Guards Heavy Tank Brigade fought at several key engagements including Kursk, Korsun, Warsaw–Posen, and Pomerania. During its final operation in Berlin the brigade ended the war near the Reichstag, having been given the honorable designation *Korsunskaya*, and awarded the Order of the Red Banner for heroism in combat on July 8, 1944.

ORDER OF BATTLE, 11th GUARDS HEAVY TANK BRIGADE, FEBRUARY 15, 1945

Actual armor strengths are underlined as xx; TO&E/KStN values for armor and manpower are not.

Commander: Colonel Boris Romanovich Eremeev
Total strength: 65/25; 1,666 men
Brigade HQ: 2/not known
HQ Company (Reconnaissance, Engineer, Chemical Defence, Signal Platoons, Supply Sections)
90th (21/14), 91st (21/6), 92nd (21/5) Guards Heavy Tank Regiments (each 375 men)
Regimental HQ (inc. Staff (1/not known), Signal, Maintenance, Reconnaissance Sections)
4 Heavy Tank Companies (each with two platoons of two IS-2s each plus one IS-2 command tank)
Submachine-Gun, Combat Engineer, Pontoon Companies
Regimental Aid Post
11th Motorized Submachine-gun Battalion (403 men)
Battalion HQ (inc. Antitank Rifle Platoon)
Submachine-Gun Company
Submachine-Gun ("*desant*"), Mortar (mot.), Antitank, Maintenance Companies

THE ACTION

POMERANIA

To bolster German defenses along the Oder River and east of Stargard, specifically against Bogdanov's Second Guards Tank Army as it rampaged across southern Pomerania, 503rd Heavy SS Panzer Battalion was activated at its bases around Berlin on January 25, 1945. With so many trained crews having been sent to the 501st and 502nd Heavy SS Panzer Battalions over the last few weeks, the formation was hard-pressed to provide occupants for its Tiger IIs when word suddenly came that it was to depart for the front line between Friedberg and Schneidemühl. As additional crews were procured the battalion's new commander, SS-Sturmbannführer Friedrich "Fritz" Herzig, implemented final preparations to enter the fray the following day.

On January 26, after months of intensive training, and having received their final shipment of 13 Tiger IIs from the Heereszeugamt (Army Ordnance Department) at Kassel, 503rd Heavy SS Panzer Battalion entrained for the short ride to the Eastern Front with 39 vehicles. Although doctrine dictated the desirability of allocating such units as a whole to maximize their battlefield potency, the number of threatened sectors along the porous Pomeranian front line pressured German commanders into parceling elements off as circumstances dictated. As the battalion passed through Berlin its 2nd Company's 1st Platoon was diverted to the Küstrin bridgehead defense as the remainder of Herzig's command continued on.

Over the next few days the Germans continued to rush forces to Pomerania to establish some sense of order. The unexpectedly rapid Soviet advance across Poland, often with accompanying turncoat Germans fighting under the *Nationalkomitee Freies*

This IS-2 is a victim of a German handheld antitank weapon such as a *Panzerfaust*. Judging by the cupola smoke the IS-2 succumbed to an internal explosion and fire. (DML)

Deutschland banner, had overwhelmed the defenders. To supplement the depleted front-line defenders, a variety of local groups were thrown together and sent into combat, such as Major Günter Kaldrack's 400 NCO cadets from Arnswalde's Panzergrenadier School, which fought near Driesen. Not surprisingly these formations suffered heavy casualties, but their efforts helped slow the overextended Soviet spearheads, and bought badly needed time, however minimal.

As 503rd Heavy SS Panzer Battalion entered their assigned sector east of Stargard on the 28th the amorphous front line added to the confusion as the formation's platoons spread out to strengthen the area's defenses. After being allocated to Generalmajor Oskar Munzel's command, Herzig accompanied his Headquarters Company and a dozen Tiger IIs as they were detrained at the Pomeranian district capital at Arnswalde. The remainder of 503rd Heavy SS Panzer Battalion pushed ahead along the northern edge of the Warthe River. Six vehicles from 3rd Panzer Company were shuttled further south toward Friedberg, while three more continued on to Schneidemühl. The remaining Tiger IIs comprised SS-Obersturmführer Max Lippert's 1st Panzer Company east of Reetz.

With Red Army forces having crossed the Warthe River at Landsberg and Driesen, 3rd Panzer Company battlegroup continued southward to help contain the latter's bridgehead. With Soviet armored patrols expected in the area, the Tiger IIs were ordered by the local commander, Generalmajor Kurt Hauschulz, to detrain prematurely west of Friedberg and continue toward their destination under their own power. As head of Sixteenth Army's NCO School at Stargard, he had recently rushed some 800 of his cadets to counter Soviet penetrations between Arnswalde and Schneidemühl. The latter, part of the pre-1939 border fortifications that stretched from north of the town to along the Warthe River, had recently been refurbished by groups including the civil/military construction outfit Organization Todt. Unfortunately for the Germans, the "Pomeranian Wall" had little more than scattered, low-quality Volkssturm militia

SS-STURMBANNFÜHRER FRIEDRICH "FRITZ" HERZIG

"Fritz" Herzig was born on July 18, 1915 in the industrial town of Wiener Neustadt, Austria, near the Hungarian border. On February 20, 1933, shortly after Hitler became Chancellor of Germany, Herzig's nearly three-month probation for acceptance into the SS ended and he was made an SS-Mann. After promotion to SS-Rottenführer he joined the Party's newly created paramilitary /combat element, SS-Verfügungstruppe (SS-VT), as part of 5th Company, II Battalion, *Deutschland* Regiment under SS-Brigadeführer Felix Steiner, on October 23, 1934. A year-long stint at the new SS-Junkerschule (Officer School) in Braunschweig was followed by additional service with *Deutschland* until mid-1939.

When war broke out with Poland, SS-Obersturmführer Herzig was the ordnance officer for SS Artillery Regiment SS-VT. On October 1, 1940 he was made commander of 3rd Company, 5th SS Motorcycle Reconnaissance Battalion, as part of Nordische Division (Nr. 5) (known as SS Infantry Division (mot.) *Wiking* after December 21, 1940, when Steiner merged SS-VT Regiment *Germania* with the Flemish and Dutch volunteers of *Westland* and the Norwegians, Swedes, and Danes of *Nordland*). Following staff work with *Das Reich*'s 2nd Regiment throughout 1942, Herzig, now an SS-Hauptsturmführer, was given command of the division's 8th (Heavy) Company of Tiger Is. From May 1943 to August 1944 Herzig's military career continued to focus on armored commands, and related training and instruction duties.

With experienced commanders needed at the front, Herzig was sent to the staff of SS Panzer Brigade *Gross*

where the formation attempted to keep Soviet forces out of Riga and the Kurland Peninsula. Five months later SS-Sturmbannführer Herzig accepted his final command with 503rd Heavy SS Panzer Battalion, which he led from Arnswalde to the fall of Berlin. After days of desperate fighting in the German capital, Herzig won the Knight's Cross for destroying eight Soviet tanks. By May 2, 1945, with all of his Tiger IIs destroyed or immobilized, he led what was left of his command from the Reich Air Ministry, and crossed the Elbe River to US lines.

Considered an effective commander by his men, Herzig was often distant and impersonal. His devotion to the cause, and bravery on the battlefield, were not doubted, as evidenced by his numerous political, combat, and sports awards. Herzig survived the war only to be killed in an automobile crash less than nine years later.

SS-Sturmbannführer "Fritz" Herzig, commander of 503rd Heavy SS Panzer Battalion. Displayed medals include the Iron Cross (both classes), Wound, and Panzer Assault Badges. (Courtesy Military Antiques of Stockholm AB)

units with which to defend it, the majority of fortress units having been sent to defend the Westwall (Siegfried Line) against British and American encroachment. Not surprisingly Soviet advances from the south and east quickly made these defenses untenable. The six-vehicle battlegroup would soon fight off Soviet armored probes and antitank positions around Heidekavel, and disrupt what supplies were moving through the area en route to Second Guards Tank Army at the Oder. Additional enemy units, however, soon forced the over-extended Germans to pull back.

With the remainder of 503rd Heavy SS Panzer Battalion deployed east of Arnswalde, Himmler ordered a portion to organize blocking positions northeast of Reetz against expected Soviet probes. A half-dozen Tiger IIs from Lippert's 1st Panzer Company set off against sporadic resistance toward the Driesen bridgehead with one of the antiaircraft platoon's three 4 × 20mm Flakpanzer IV *Wirbelwind* self-propelled guns. Along with 365 grounded paratroopers from Fallschirmjäger Regiment zbV (special employment) *Schlacht* the battlegroup merged with elements of a reconnaissance and an antiaircraft battalion at Neuwedell before heading south to win back the recently Soviet-occupied town of Regenthin.

Further east, 2nd Company's 3rd Platoon deployed three of its four Tiger IIs and the battalion's antiaircraft platoon at Schneidemühl. With one Tiger II soon succumbing to mechanical problems, the remaining vehicles moved to the eastern edge of town at Bromberger. Soviet artillery steadily shelled the surrounding area from the nearby Schneidemühl Forest as the two Tiger IIs established "hull down" positions behind a protective railway embankment. Leaving the immobilized tank to fight in the forthcoming siege of Schneidemühl, what was left of 2nd Company's 3rd Platoon was ordered to return to the west to help defend Küstrin. With a small contingent of protective infantry hitching a ride the group avoided Soviet patrols as they made their way past Friedberg and Landsberg to reach their 180km-distant destination on January 30.

On January 29 Generalmajor Hans Voigt was reallocated from his duties as Commandant of the "Pomeranian Wall" fortresses to that of "*Festung Arnswalde*" to organize a motley collection of nearby units. Along with Kaldrack's remaining cadets, Battalion *Enge* and Replacement Staff for Artillery Regiment zV ("for retribution"), recently freed from their V-2 rocket-launching duties, provided 400 and 800 fighters, respectively, for Arnswalde's defense. Possessing little more than small arms and a few machine guns these groups were bolstered by two Volkssturm battalions, a Landesschützen (Territorial Defense) battalion, and a detachment from 83rd Light Antiaircraft Battalion that provided two antiaircraft batteries, a 20mm battery, and a

Even the 70-tonne Tiger II could be overturned by artillery or aerial bombing. The lower glacis features Zimmerit; note the emergency escape panel under the radio operator's compartment and the smaller drain cocks used for purging used oil and other liquids. (DML)

55

37mm self-propelled Flakpanzer IV *Ostwind*. With only a handful of 81mm mortars and no artillery, Voigt's command relied on hand-held antitank weapons and machine guns to provide support, as the former V-2 staff members established security positions at Hohenwalde, Klücken, Kürtow, and Zühlsdorf.

To the east the 1st Panzer Company battlegroup recaptured Neuwedell, but the effort resulted in high losses among the Fallschirmjäger. With a mix of NCO cadets, Volkssturm, emergency, and other units under 402nd Division Staff zbV providing support Lippert set out the following day with his available paratroopers and four Tiger IIs some 10km toward Regenthin. Numerous Soviet antitank guns and infantry, however, forced the Germans to withdraw to avoid being cut off.

St Mary's Church was built in Arnswalde's central marketplace by the Knights of St John in the 14th century. As with most of the town's structures, the gothic structure was heavily damaged during the 1945 siege. (Courtesy Jarosław Piotrowski)

SOVIET DEPLOYMENTS

Since pushing west from their bridgehead along the Vistula River on January 16, Colonel Boris Eremeev's 11th Guards Heavy Tank Brigade made excellent progress as it punched through German defenses ahead of the now ubiquitous T-34/85 medium tanks and mechanized forces. Increasingly urbanized combat and lengthening supply lines took a mechanical toll on the IS-2s, which were routinely doubling their design-estimated battlefield lives. Second Guards Tank Army, for example, lost 52 percent of their tanks and self-propelled guns to enemy armor and artillery, and 43 percent to German handheld antitank weapons such as the *Panzerfaust* and *Panzerschreck* in the first 24 days of the Vistula–Oder Offensive. As a defense against the latter, Soviet tankers began to apply makeshift screens made from found materials such as sheet metal, tank tracks, and wire mesh. As shaped-charge weapons needed to impact armor at a set distance to impart maximum destruction, these "bed springs" acted to prematurely dissipate the narrow 500°C jet before it contacted the vehicle's main armor. Without them the crew risked being engulfed in a molten inferno that externally left a scorched hole dubbed a "witch's kiss."

As the Replacement Staff for Artillery Regiment zV constricted to new positions at Hohenwalde, Karlsaue, Karlsburg, Wardin, and Helpe, the Soviet 88th Guards Heavy Tank Regiment (five IS-2s), 85th Individual Tank Regiment (eight T-34/85s), 43 open-topped SU-76 self-propelled guns, and motorized artillery began moving into the area. Just behind, IX Guards Rifle Corps and XVIII Rifle Corps pushed north, but XII Guards Tank Corps was running out of fuel and only allocated enough for combat and staff vehicles, and a few motor transports.

Tiger IIs knocked out several enemy tanks around Schönwerder, while more such attacks occurred south of Arnswalde. Intent on their own survival many Party officials and the police abandoned Arnswalde for Reetz. Voigt, understandably incensed by the abandonment of the civilians, did what he could to get them out of the enveloping perimeter before it was too late. By the end of the day Tiger IIs repulsed enemy probes near Neuwedell, where 503rd Heavy SS Panzer Battalion's Workshop Company was located to be close to the fighting.

After several days of frosty weather, February 3 brought warmer temperatures and a thaw that softened ground and made movement increasingly difficult, especially for motorized formations. Southwest of Arnswalde at Sammenthin Tiger IIs rescued some surrounded infantry at Kopplinsthal, and four vehicles from 1st Panzer Company continued on to bolster Arnswalde's defenses at Hohenwalde. Three Tiger IIs were damaged by heavy enemy armor and antitank fire. The remaining four vehicles fought near a wooded area at Sammenthin, where at 0700hrs the following morning Tiger 111 was destroyed and SS-Untersturmführer Karl Brommann's vehicle (221) was immobilized by antitank fire and towed by three Tiger IIs to the Evangelical St Mary's Church in the center of Arnswalde. Armored train No. 77 from Group *Munzel* provided intermittent local support, but when the Soviets overran the tracks east of Reetz later on February 4 it was forced from the area.

ARNSWALDE ENCIRCLED

With Soviet forces having reached the Ihna River southwest of Zachen, Steiner ordered Group *Munzel* to strengthen Arnswalde's defenses. On February 6 the *Nordland* Division sent in 15 Sturmgeschütze (assault guns) from 11th SS Assault Gun Battalion and SS-Obersturmbannführer Paul-Albert "Peter" Kausch's 11th SS Panzer Battalion *Hermann von Salza*, which held off advancing enemy forces around Reetz. Soviet pressure on either flank, however, proved irresistible as masses of refugees tried to extricate themselves. When the Arnswalde–Reetz road was severed later in the day upwards of 5,000 refugees were trapped within the Arnswalde perimeter. Heavy Soviet artillery made the situation seem all the more hopeless, and Voigt considered capitulation, but did not act on it. In preparation for a rescue of the Arnswalde garrison SS-Untersturmführer Fritz Kauerauf (commander of 2nd Platoon, 1st Panzer Company) was ordered to take three repaired Tiger IIs from the battalion workshop now at Stargard.

ARNSWALDE'S GARRISON

503rd Heavy SS Panzer Battalion (seven Tiger IIs; Company HQ)
Artillery Regiment zbV *Hohmann*
83rd Light Antiaircraft Battalion (20mm single and quad guns)
Urlauber Battalion (comprised of soldiers returning from leave)

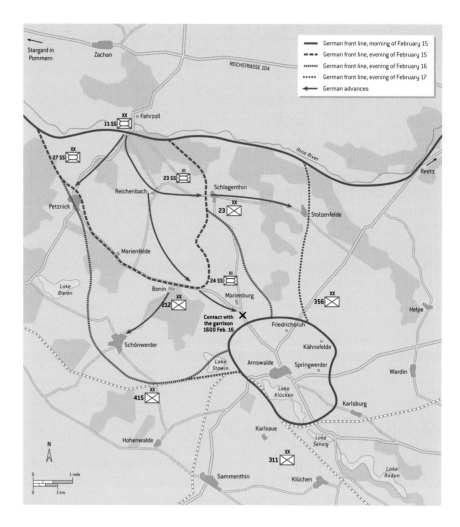

A tactical view of the relief of the Arnswalde garrison, February 15–17, 1945.

Escort Battalion zbV *Reichsführer-SS* (Gross) (HQ; Signals Platoon; Engineer Platoon; 1st, 2nd and 3rd Schützen Companies; Heavy Machine Gun Company; Heavy Company)

Urlauber Company (from Arnswalde)

Army Standortverwaltung (local administration)

The next day Soviet forces pushed back the roughly 1,000-member Dutch brigade, soon re-christened as the loftily titled 23rd SS Volunteer Panzergrenadier Division *Nederland*, overran Reetz and Hassendorf, and cut Reichsstrasse 104 to Stettin. Considerable Soviet forces, including armor and artillery, snaked their way north along the ridgeline just east of the Ihna River north of Reetz.

At dawn on February 8 Kausch ordered Kauerauf to send one of his Tiger IIs from 1st Platoon, 3rd Panzer Company, and three Sturmgeschütze under the very experienced SS-Obersturmführer Hermann Wild to report on Soviet activity north of Reetz. After moving from Kausch's headquarters south of Jakobshagen the group crested the high ground just west of Ziegenhagen and saw a seemingly endless enemy

This German soldier sets a German hollow-charge Hafthohlladung 3 antitank magnetic mine in a T-34's visibility "dead zone" during training. Designed to be placed at an optimal 90 degrees, this mine's shaped-charge design defeated armor in the same way as the rounds fired from handheld weapons such as the US bazooka and the German *Panzerfaust* and *Panzerschreck*. (NARA)

column of armor, artillery, and infantry passing through Klein Silber, which if left unchecked threatened to move on to the Baltic coast and cut German forces still moving by land into Pomerania from the east. Wild went for reinforcements, and soon returned with two Tiger IIs, ten additional Sturmgeschütze from Battalion *Herman von Salza*, and a Fallschirmjäger company as a force with which to eliminate the enemy thrust.

After quickly organizing from the march, the German battlegroup halted to fire on several Soviet antitank guns west of Ziegenhagen around noon. As per the semi-informal *Tigerfibel* (Tiger Manual), crews were to maintain controlled fire and limit unnecessary ammunition expenditure by being like boxer (and Fallschirmjäger member) "Max Schmeling's right" and not to use shells until the moment of truth. As Fallschirmjäger moved up on either side of the road past Ziegenhagen and across a bridge into Klein Silber, a pair of Sturmgeschütze led a Tiger II through the latter town amid heavy small arms fire. The assault guns were soon stopped by a Soviet antitank gun near a church some 200m away, but a ridge in no-man's land obscured each side and forced their fire high.

Kauerauf was apprised of the impasse and moved his taller Tiger II into a hull-down position to knock out the surprised enemy gun crew with a Sprgr 43 HE round. As the German armor began to move on, Kauerauf was soon halted by a hastily laid enemy minefield in the street. The Fallschirmjäger fought their way forward, but with no engineers available one of the paratroopers rushed forward to destroy the mines with grenades and demolition charges. No sooner was the street cleared than a Soviet IS-2 came into view at 50m, which Kauerauf disabled with a Pzgr 39/43 antitank projectile, finishing it off with two more such hits. Two more IS-2s ground to a halt nearby after seeing Kauerauf's results and simply abandoned their vehicles and disappeared. With the Red Army's northward advance through Klein Silber now severed the trio of Tiger IIs formed a defensive hedgehog formation along the village's

German soldiers in training position a strip of five Tellermine 35 antitank mines against a T-34 Model 1941 (note the "blackout" headlight covers, early tow shackles, and "plate" tracks). Each mine's 5.5kg charge of TNT would certainly blow off the vehicle's track, and possibly damage its suspension and injure the crew. (NARA)

southern end to take on fuel and ammunition. Over the next day two were destroyed by Soviet infantry and a third by its crew after it became immobilized.

As the front line began to stabilize along the Ihna River's southern edge, Soviet forces focused on eliminating the Arnswalde garrison. At 1000hrs on February 9, eight Tiger IIs led ten armored personnel carriers from I Battalion, 100th Panzergrenadier Regiment, *Führer Escort* Division, from the bridgehead at Fahrzoll, but the effort to reach the town's defenders stalled. With fuel and aircraft running low, Luftflotte 6 had several of its venerable Ju-52 transports airdrop supplies to the beleaguered "fortress" during the nights of February 8/9 to 11/12, 13/14, and 14/15. Whether because of oversight or sabotage by foreign factory workers much of the ammunition replenishment for the Tiger IIs was 88mm Flak 36 rounds, which being designed for antiaircraft guns were unusable.

After the Red Army captured perhaps the most formidable section of the "Pomeranian Wall" at Deutsche Krone on the 11th, and Tiger IIs with Battalion *Gross* devastated a T-34 unit at Kähnsfelde, fighting around Arnswalde waned as both sides regrouped. To test the garrison's resolve and avoid a costly fight, the Soviets sent three German captives to Arnswalde's eastern perimeter at Springwerder during the evening of the 12th. Under a flag of truce the trio carried a message from their captors stating that to prevent unnecessary casualties the garrison needed to surrender by 0800hrs the following day. As an incentive the German defenders were told they would then be given food and medical attention, and be allowed to retain their personal effects, and civilians would simply be allowed to go their own way. But knowing the harsh fate that Germans in areas overrun by the Red Army had already experienced, there was little reason for them to expect different treatment.

At the designated time, instead of a white flag, the German defenders defiantly displayed both the German imperial and Party flags from St Mary's Church. Incensed, the Soviets unleashed an artillery, mortar, and Katyusha rocket barrage lasting over seven hours that did considerable damage to the town. To the east, Schneidemühl's garrison faced imminent destruction. Organizing into three groups each broke out for friendly lines on the 13th, but a quick Soviet response meant only a few reached their goal at Deutsche Krone. The roughly 15,000 civilians were left to the mercy of the Soviet and Polish forces that would take the city the next day. Having gathered the 1 6 operational Tiger IIs that weren't encircled, 11th SS Panzer Army commanders would do everything possible to prevent such a situation at Arnswalde. With most of III (Germanic) SS Panzer Corps having been successfully transported by sea from the Courland Peninsula, Steiner was able to position sizeable forces east of Stargard. To lead 11th SS Panzer Army's scheduled counterattack, personnel of the *Nordland* Division conducted training and familiarized themselves with the area in the days leading up to the offensive before being put on alert on February 14.

SONNENWENDE

With relatively warm temperatures continuing, intermittent rain and sleet greeted Eleventh SS Panzer Army as they prepared to go over to the offensive between Lake Madü and Hassendorf. Although Steiner favored first building his command's offensive capability, Guderian's timetable won out, and the attack was scheduled to start on the 16th. With the *Nordland* Division ready a day early its commander, SS-Brigadeführer Joachim Ziegler, met with local commanders before dawn on the 15th to discuss their coming objectives. As they had been allocated 31 Sturmgeschütz III Ausf Gs (1st, 2nd, 3rd Companies), and 30 Panther Ausf Ds (4th Company) there seemed a good chance of at least limited success.

In the gray pre-dawn the *Nordland* Division's depleted 24th SS Panzergrenadier Regiment *Danmark* moved its II Battalion up to its jump-off positions just south of the Ihna River. While they passed into 27th SS Volunteer Grenadier Division *Langemarck*'s security zone/bridgehead south of Fahrzoll *Nordland*'s 11th SS Engineer Battalion strengthened the light wooden bridge over the river to provide a crossing for the supporting German vehicles as the surrounding terrain was too soft for such movement. With I Battalion, 100th Panzergrenadier Regiment (*Führer Escort* Division) not yet prepared to support *Nordland*, Regiment *Danmark*'s Danish volunteers began their attack at 0600hrs with the intent of relieving Arnswalde's garrison as a prelude to the wider effort to sever Second Guards Tank Army's spearheads.

By noon Regiment *Danmark*'s II Battalion had recaptured Reichenbach, while their supporting tanks and *Führer Escort* Division's half-track personnel carriers crossed the Ihna River. Surprised by finding themselves on the defensive, Soviet forward elements from 212th and 23rd Rifle Divisions fell back in confusion. Exploiting the situation, elements of Battalion *Hermann von Salza* plus 11th SS Panzerjäger Battalion's 3rd Company and a platoon from that battalion's 1st Company advanced on either side of Reichenbach at 1400hrs and continued toward Marienburg. To the left the Norwegians of 23rd SS Panzergrenadier Regiment *Norge*'s II Battalion (*Nordland* Division)

OVERLEAF
A Tiger II defends the Arnswalde perimeter near Kähnsfelde. On February 10, 1945, Tiger IIs, with support from Escort Battalion zbV *Reichsführer-SS*, stopped a Soviet assault on the Arnswalde perimeter at Kähnsfelde. To make the best use of the Tiger II's long range, these vehicles were positioned along the small hills that bordered the area's low-lying, swampy terrain and its small bisecting stream, the Stübenitz. With ammunition running low the German commander had to be very selective in choosing targets. Because of their firepower and protection, IS-2s would be a primary focus, but the more numerous medium T-34/85s could not be ignored. As high-explosive rounds would not be effective in targeting enemy armor, the Sprgr Patr 43 (HE) would probably be used against infantry when a sector was threatened with being overrun.

attempted to secure the operation's northern flank, but were unable to wrest Schlagenthin away from the Soviets. By day's end companies from the *Langemarck* Division had established positions before Petznick and Regiment *Danmark* held positions near Bonin where their patrols made contact with Voigt's encircled command.

On Friday 16th, Operation *Sonnenwende* officially commenced. On the German right XXXIX Panzer Corps's *Holstein* Panzer Division and the nearly full-strength 10th SS Panzer Division *Frundsberg* burst into XII Guards Tank Corps' security zone, and pushed 34th Guards Mechanized and 48th Guards Tank Brigades back to south of Lake Madü. The *Frundsberg* Division's subsequent efforts to link up with 4th SS *Polizei* Panzergrenadier Division, which with 28th SS Volunteer Grenadier Division *Wallonien* was to form a pocket around Soviet forces between Arnswalde and the lake, came to naught. A quick and stubborn reaction by 66th Guards Tank Brigade with some 15 T-34/85s made further German progress near the area's saltworks difficult. The southern Belgians from the *Wallonien* Division, essentially a 4,000-man battlegroup, made every effort to support the *Nordland* Division's right flank, but could make little headway past Lake Plöne. Along Eleventh SS Panzer Army's left X SS Corps began its own offensive around Reetz. Using the *Führer Escort* and *Führer Grenadier* Divisions the formation made initially good progress even though confronted by considerable Soviet antitank defenses.

Comprising the primary German effort in the center, III (Germanic) SS Panzer Corps crossed the Ihna River to reinforce the *Nordland* Division's success the previous day. The Soviet VII Guards Cavalry Corps fell back in some disarray, but XVIII Rifle Corps continued to maintain its grip around Arnswalde. Until greater numbers of heavy Soviet artillery could be redirected northward, the front line was not likely to solidify any time soon. Sixty-First Army commander Colonel-General Belov moved to reduce the Arnswalde garrison before the Germans could break the siege by sending two heavy tank regiments from 11th Guards Heavy Tank Brigade to the area as a breakthrough element for 356th and 212th Rifle Divisions. Having only 260 and 300 soldiers available for action, respectively, the force was in poor shape to undertake such a mission. 85th Tank and 1899th Self-Propelled Artillery Regiments were subsequently moved up to provide armored support for a re-implemented attack that included 311th and 415th Rifle Divisions once they arrived on the scene.

Tiger IIs from 503rd Heavy SS Panzer Battalion were able to effectively engage enemy armor at long range, but the recent thaw had created very muddy terrain that hindered movement. The Germans knew that if the ground will support a man standing on one leg and carrying another man on his shoulders, it will support a tank. Although considerably reduced in strength by recent fighting along the Baltic coast, the *Nordland* Division continued to fight through sporadic Soviet resistance. Retaining the element of surprise, German forces exploited the situation to resolve their mission as quickly as possible in spite of environmental conditions unsuited for armored operations.

In response to the broader *Sonnenwende* operation Soviet commanders activated several local IS-2 formations for a counterattack. Lieutenant-Colonel Joseph Rafailovich's 70th Guards Heavy Tank Regiment (Forty-Seventh Army) was positioned north of Woldenberg, while Lieutenant-Colonel Semen Kalabukhov's

79th (XII Guards Tank Corps) assembled near Dölitz. Lieutenant-Colonel Peter Grigorevich's 88th Guards Heavy Tank Regiment was also available near Berlinchen in Sixty-First Army's sector.

Regiment *Danmark*'s III Battalion was ordered to take Bonin with support from *Führer Escort* Division's mounted Panzergrenadiers and three Sturmgeschütze from the *Nordland* Division. On establishing a defensive position south of the village and the nearby Volkswagen factory the half-tracks and assault guns turned for Schönwerder to assist Regiment *Danmark*'s II Battalion. I Battalion, 66th SS Grenadier Regiment (*Langemarck* Division) launched a concurrent attack with Regiment *Danmark*'s III Battalion's effort to take Marienfelde and establish a combat outpost at Petznick. Following these assaults, Regiment *Danmark*'s II Battalion was to capture Schönwerder, while Regiment *Norge* captured Schlagenthin and pushed outposts to Stolzenfelde to anchor the corridor's left flank.

At 1600hrs parts of Regiment *Danmark* broke from their positions at Bonin and captured Schönwerder in a quick assault. As additional companies reinforced the success, the remainder of the battalion weathered XVIII Rifle Corps' artillery fire to reach Arnswalde's northwestern perimeter and break the 11-day siege with a defensible corridor. Seven Tiger IIs that had been attached to the *Nordland* Division soon entered the town along with other reinforcements that proceeded to strengthen the garrison's defenses. As the Germans expanded the corridor, strong enemy resistance along the Stargard–Arnswalde railroad stopped further progress in that area. To the north contact was made with parts of Regiment *Danmark*'s III Battalion along the tracks with friendly units at Marienburg.

On the 17th, Second Guards Tank Army arrived in force in the Arnswalde sector and stopped what little impetus the *Frundsberg* and *Polizei* Divisions retained. While the latter tried to work into the flank and rear of XII Guards Rifle Corps and 75th Rifle Division, 6th Guards Heavy Tank Regiment moved up to counter the effort.

A front view of a well-used IS-2 that appears to have suffered damage along the side of the hull. As an early "broken-nose" model it has a narrow mantlet. Note the missing tow shackle and the other IS-2 to the right. (DML)

The *Wallonien* Division continued to hold on to their positions in the Linden Hills, with one company fighting nearly to the last man against repeated enemy assaults.

Around Arnswalde, 14 IS-2s from Hero of the Soviet Union Major Prokofi Kalashnikov's 90th Guards Heavy Tank Regiment moved up to join the already-in-action 91st and 92nd with six and five IS-2s respectively, but success remained elusive. 356th Rifle Division managed to get infantry elements into the suburbs near the city's gas works, but German infantry firing from the upper floors of buildings, and roaming Tiger IIs, made infiltration impossible.

TIGER II GUNSIGHT

A Tiger II gunner uses his TZF 9d sight to target an IS-2 as it is resupplied by a US Lend/Lease supply truck at 1,800m

Fine-tuning his aim from 2.5× to 5× magnification, the gunner prepares to fire a PzGr Patr 39/43 APCBC/HE-T round into the unsuspecting enemy vehicle's thinner side armor

Here we see the view through a Tiger II's TZF 9d gunsight targeting an IS-2 as it and another are resupplied by a Lend/Lease supply truck. Believing themselves to be safely out of enemy range, the two halted IS-2s take on supplies and fuel before moving up for an attack. Soviet support personnel go about their business next to an American IHC M-5-6×4-318 supply truck. When the Soviets went over to the strategic offensive in 1943, foreign-provided Lend/Lease equipment and vehicles such as this one greatly assisted with logistics.

The Tiger II's firing sequence proceeds similarly to that on the IS-2. With a projectile ready in the breech, and if the target is beyond some 500m, the gunner estimates the target's actual size and divides it by the number of mills it encompasses in the 'scope. The loader adjusts the tick marks on the *Turmzielfernrohr* 9d monocular gunsight in accordance with both the selected ammunition and the range, the latter being agreed upon by the driver, gunner, and commander. Once it is rotated so that the large black triangle at the 'scope's top points to the estimated range, the upper tip of the large central triangle atop the vertical line is located between the targeted IS-2's turret and hull.

With a stable corridor out of Arnswalde now available Voigt quickly orchestrated the evacuation of the civilians and wounded. Although briefly severed, Soviet efforts to permanently eliminate the 2km-wide corridor were unsuccessful. Of the original seven garrison Tiger IIs, only four remained operational. Battered and in need of maintenance, the vehicles were withdrawn to Zachan.

Just after midnight on the 18th the commander of the German offensive was seriously injured in a car accident. While returning to the front following a briefing at the Reich Chancellery, Wenck had taken the wheel from his driver, who had also

IS-2 GUNSIGHT

The view through an IS-2's TSh-17 gunsight targeting a defending German Tiger II at 800m

Using one of their eight BR-471 armor-piercing rounds, the Soviet crew scores a hit against the target's frontal armor

In an effort to penetrate the defensive line around Arnswalde, Soviet infantry move forward in a dispersed formation to minimize casualties. Receiving small-arms and mortar fire, many of the attackers have fallen but the remainder continue on through smoke and churned earth. The attackers wear the M1940 steel helmet or *shapka-ushanka* synthetic pile winter cap, as well as khaki padded *telogreika* jackets and greatcoats.

The forward German positions extend around the outskirts of the town, with trenches and foxholes placed so as to make the best use of terrain. This line is manned by infantry and reinforced by the occasional machine-gun crew. To their rear a Tiger II, partly camouflaged by rubble and earth, provides support.

Once the IS-2 commander has called out a target type and location, the loader assembles the proper round and charge and positions it within the breech. The IS-2's gunner correspondingly uses the TSh-17 gunsight to estimate range by using the angled mill marks. Once the range is determined the horizontal line is positioned at the correct "БРОГ" scale for armor-piercing rounds, or the "ДТ" for the coaxial DT machine gun and high-explosive rounds, with the arrow's tip placed over the target. Crews seldom fired on enemy armor beyond 1,200m as it accomplished little save exposing the IS-2's firing position.

been on duty for over two days straight, only to fall asleep himself. Suffering from a fractured skull and broken ribs, Wenck was replaced by Generalleutnant Hans Krebs, but the offensive's momentum could not be maintained.

EVACUATION

In Arnswalde, Voigt met with the new commander of III (Germanic) SS Panzer Corps, Generalleutnant Martin Unrein, to discuss the deteriorating situation and withdrawal from their extended positions. Unrein, having taken over on February 10 after recovering from an illness, found himself in the unusual position of an Army commander of Waffen-SS forces. Seeing that further efforts would not alter the failure of *Sonnenwende* he agreed to let Voigt extricate his command from Arnswalde. Soviet pressure to the east and west of the town threatened to collapse Voigt's battle zone and close combat was already occurring in parts of the town, but III (Germanic) SS Panzer Corps' artillery helped keep Soviet forces at bay throughout the day.

After sunset civilians and wounded began to evacuate Arnswalde and move back along Regiment *Danmark*'s route to Zachan some 20km to the northwest, where trucks waited to take as many as they could west. With *Sonnenwende* nearing its unsuccessful end 503rd Heavy SS Panzer Battalion received orders that it was to be transferred to the fight raging around Danzig and Gotenhafen. Although heavy fighting flared up around Arnswalde's military base and near the railroad station, self-propelled antitank guns from 1st Company, 11th SS Panzerjäger Battalion, moved in to support the town's defenders, while the exodus from the combat zone continued.

For the *Nordland* Division, February 18 was relatively quiet, but reconnaissance indicated a strong enemy buildup west of the Stargard–Arnswalde railroad. Another company from the *Langemarck* Division was inserted between Marienfelde and Regiment *Danmark*'s II Battalion to reinforce the area. German offensive activity had to stop due to increasing Soviet pressure, and Himmler called an end to *Sonnenwende* the following morning.

On February 19, Zhukov initiated his planned offensive aimed at capturing Stettin using the Sixty-First and Second Guards Tank Armies as well as the VII Guards Cavalry Corps, which remained embroiled in heavy street fighting at Arnswalde. With Soviet pressure threatening once again to encircle the town and destroy its defenders, Voigt and Ziegler developed a plan to evacuate their fighting elements from the town. A Soviet armored assault comprised of T-34/85s, IS-2s, and KV-1s was repulsed 3km northeast of Arnswalde at Friedrichsruh. Throughout the day Regiment *Norge* and Regiment *Danmark* were subjected to enemy artillery that included multi-barreled "Stalin's Organs" as they rebuffed Soviet probes toward Schönwerder.

Belov ordered 23rd Rifle Division to go over to the offensive after relieving VII Guards Cavalry Corps. XVIII Rifle Corps was to cease its assault on Arnswalde's perimeter, and attain a defensive stance, although Soviet assault teams within the town were allowed to continue their activity. What IS-2s were in support were forced to operate with their hatches closed to minimize damage from hand grenades and handheld antitank weapons, many of which were being used from higher building elevations. To compensate for the loss of visibility and control in the urban environment "herringbone" tactics were used, in which a four-vehicle platoon would be divided into two pairs of tanks. In what was basically a variation of fire-and-movement, the first pair would advance along a street with each vehicle focusing to the right and left, respectively. From a stationary position to the rear, the remaining two IS-2s provided supporting fire.

To improve tactical flexibility and success, each tank company was allocated a submachine-gun platoon. These infantrymen rode the tanks into action, and dismounted to ferret out German *Panzerfaust* hunter/killer teams, and other resistance. To further motivate the destruction of enemy armor, NKO issued order No. 0387 on June 24, 1943, to pay out 500 rubles to the tank commanders and drivers, and 200 rubles to the loaders and gunners, of the vehicles responsible for a kill. Artillery and antitank crews received similar bonuses, which eventually increased to 1,000 rubles for individuals single-handedly accomplishing the task.

By February 20 Group *Munzel* and Voigt's command managed to get all their civilian charges and wounded out of the combat zone without incident, due in no small part to the *Nordland* Division's constant struggle to keep the corridor open, a feat seldom accomplished to any great degree at other "fortress" cities. The next day German artillery kept Soviet forces at bay, while the garrison made final preparations to disengage from their perimeter defenses and withdraw back to III (Germanic) SS Panzer Corps' former positions along the Ihna River. The other forces involved in *Sonnenwende* were similarly pulled back, or remained in positions perceived as defensible, so as to make it appear that at least one military objective was

Placing a makeshift Stielhandgranate 24/gas-filled jerry can improvised explosive on the engine deck of enemy armor was one of several tank destruction methods listed in the German manual called *Die Panzerknacker* ("the armor cracker"). The victim here is a T-34 Model 1941 with early rubber-rimmed road wheels. (NARA)

A section of the Stargard–Arnswalde railroad about 3km west of the latter. After taking Schönwerder on the 16th, elements from 11th SS-Panzergrenadier Division *Nordland* pushed past 212th and 415th Rifle Divisions and expanded the recently created corridor to Arnswalde. (Courtesy Mariusz Gajowniczek)

accomplished. German units that had participated in *Sonnenwende* began to be pulled from the sector to regroup or be redirected to other threatened areas.

Regiment *Norge* and Regiment *Danmark* received orders to the effect that with the *Nordland* Division's flanks so extended, the corridor to Arnswalde could not be maintained, and that the front would soon be pulled back. Petznick was never taken by the *Langemarck* Division. At 1700hrs the first of three groups of defenders began their march northwest out of Arnswalde's defenses. The remainder followed at 1800 and 1900hrs, with SS-Sturmbannführer Heinz-Dieter Gross leading the rearguard at 2000hrs. After 15 days of combat, Voigt's command quietly and efficiently left their positions without arousing enemy suspicions.

Just before midnight Regiment *Danmark*'s II and III Battalions began to withdraw back to Bonin, with the latter acting as a regimental rear guard and observation force for another day. Four hours later Soviet artillery fell on Schönwerder, which unknown to the Soviets had already been abandoned. At dawn forward Soviet units discovered that the Germans had left the immediate combat zone and began a cautious approach north to regain contact. At noon on the 22nd VII Cavalry Corps elements were repulsed at Bonin.

At 2200hrs that night Regiment *Danmark*'s II Battalion continued to hold its position at Petznick to act as flank protection for the Fahrzoll bridgehead as *Danmark*'s III Battalion crossed the Ihna. About 45 minutes later Regiment *Norge*'s III Battalion pulled out of Schlagenthin and crossed as well, followed by *Danmark*'s II Battalion. When the final German unit, *Norge*'s 10th Company, moved to the river's north bank the recently reinforced bridge to Zachan was blown up.

Starting on February 23, Zhukov's commitment of the Seventieth Army into an attack spurred a general German retreat from along the Ihna River. As the Germans had not received orders to pre-empt such a situation and establish new defenses to the rear many vehicles and equipment had to be abandoned. Two days later Red Army forces captured an abandoned Arnswalde. With 1st Belorussian Front now assisting Rokossovsky in clearing Pomerania, it would be another six weeks before the Soviets would initiate their long-awaited offensive against Berlin.

STATISTICS AND ANALYSIS

Although service in an armored vehicle would seemingly impart a reduced physical risk compared to infantry and artillery units that were not protected against bullets, shrapnel, and weather, tank crewmen faced their own hazards. While World War II infantry suffered higher physical casualties, tankers were afflicted with a greater incidence of mental disorders related to working and fighting in a hot claustrophobic environment where direct contact with the outside world was limited. Constant vibration caused knee and back problems, edema (fluid pooling), muscle atrophy, and radiculitis (spinal nerve inflammation). Explosions from antitank mines or forceful, non-penetrating projectile impacts could cause blunt trauma and shower the interior with spall. Carbon monoxide buildup was especially problematic, especially when the vehicle was "buttoned up" with its hatches closed. Noise was an ever-present problem during operation, where those exposed to constant noise exceeding 85dB hearing damage. With the firing of main guns and movement often producing 140dB and between 120dB and 200dB respectively, effective communication and target detection was often hampered due to crew disorientation.

THE TIGER II

While medium armored fighting vehicles such as the German Panther or Soviet T-34 possessed a balanced triad of firepower, mobility, and protection that permitted them to undertake a variety of combat roles, the Tiger II's greater weight relegated it to

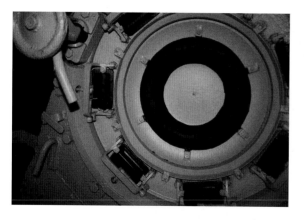

This interior view of a Tiger II's cupola shows the hatch wheel/lever (at upper left). The seven brackets held replaceable glass vision blocks should they become damaged. (Author's collection)

more limited defensive operations. Its size made movement through urban environments or along narrow roads difficult, while its drivetrain was under-strength, the double radius L801 steering gear was stressed, and the seals and gaskets were prone to leaks. Limited crew training could amplify these problems as inexperienced drivers could inadvertently run the engine at high RPMs or move over terrain that overly tasked the suspension. Extended travel times under the Tiger II's own power stressed the swingarms that supported the road wheels and made them susceptible to bending. Such axial displacement would probably strain the tracks and bend the link bolts to further disrupt proper movement. Over-worked engines needed to be replaced roughly every 1,000km. Although wide tracks aided movement over most terrain, should the vehicle require recovery another Tiger II was typically needed to extract it. Requirements for spare parts were understandably high, and maintenance was an ongoing task, all of which reduced vehicle availability.

The Tiger II's long main armament, the epitome of the family of 88mm antiaircraft/antitank guns that had terrorized enemy armor since the Spanish Civil War (1936–39), fired high-velocity rounds along a relatively flat trajectory. In combination with an excellent gunsight, the weapon system was accurate at long range, which enabled rapid targeting and a high first look/first hit/first kill probability. However, the lengthy barrel's overhang stressed the turret ring, and made traverse difficult when not on level ground. Optimally initiating combat at distances beyond which an enemy's main armament could effectively respond, the Tiger II's lethality was further enhanced by its considerable armor protection, especially across the frontal arc that provided for a high degree of combat survivability. Although the vehicle's glacis does not appear to have ever been penetrated during battle, its flanks and rear were vulnerable to enemy antitank weapons at normal ranges.

In the hands of an experienced crew, and under environmental and terrain conditions that promoted long-range combat, the weapon system achieved a high kill ratio against its Allied and Red Army counterparts. 503rd Heavy SS Panzer Battalion, for example, was estimated to have scored an estimated 500 "kills" during the unit's operational life from January to April 1945. While such a figure was certainly inflated as accurate record keeping was hindered by the unit's dispersed application and chaotic late-war fighting where the Soviets eventually occupied a battlefield, it illustrated the success of the weapon system if properly employed and supported. Of 503rd Heavy SS Panzer Battalion's original complement of 39 Tiger IIs only ten were destroyed through combat, with the remainder being abandoned or destroyed by their crews due to mechanical breakdowns or lack of fuel. As 503rd Heavy SS Panzer Battalion never received replacement tanks like its brethren in 501st and 502nd Heavy SS Panzer Battalions (which were given 2.38 and 1.7 times their respective 45-vehicle TO&E allotments), its Tiger II combat losses averaged less than 50 percent.

An IS-2 with a welded, streamlined glacis and a 12.7mm DShK 1938 antiaircraft machine gun. The photograph appears to have been retouched at the end of the gun barrel, either to obscure the background or to emphasize the muzzle brake. [DML]

Because of the chaotic combat environment throughout Pomerania, and the need to quickly allocate resources to several threatened sectors at once, the Tiger IIs were frequently employed singly, or in small groups, often at the will of a local senior commander. In much the same way as with the French in 1940, 503rd Heavy SS Panzer Battalion's armor acted more in an infantry-support capacity than as a unified armored fist. The Tiger IIs would perhaps have been better used organizationally to fill a Panzer regiment's heavy company by strengthening existing, depleted parent formations; but instead they remained in semi-independent heavy Panzer battalions until the end of the war. Forced to rely on small-unit tactics, Tiger II crews played to their strengths by adopting ambush tactics to minimize vehicular movement and pre-combat detection, especially from enemy ground-attack aircraft.

As tankers regularly spent long hours in their mounts the Tiger II's relatively spacious interior helped reduce fatigue, and made operating and fighting within the vehicle somewhat less taxing. A good heating and ventilation system improved operating conditions, which then reduced crew mistakes that were all too common during a chaotic firefight. Although the Tiger II had well-positioned ammunition racks that facilitated loading, projectiles that were stored in the turret bustle were susceptible to potentially catastrophic damage caused by spalling or projectile impacts. Even after Henschel incorporated spall liners to reduce such debris, concerned crews would often leave the turret rear empty, which correspondingly made room to use the rear hatch as an emergency exit.

The cost to produce the Tiger II in manpower and time (double that of a 45-tonne Panther), and its high fuel consumption, brought into question why such a design progressed beyond the drawing board considering Germany's dwindling resources and military fortunes. It was partly a response to the perpetual escalation of the requirement to achieve or maintain battlefield supremacy, and much of the blame rested with Hitler and his desire for large armored vehicles that in his view presumably reflected Germany's might and reinforced propaganda. By not focusing resources on creating greater numbers of the latest proven designs such as the Panther G, German authorities showed a lack of unified direction and squandered an ability to fight a war of attrition until it was too late to significantly affect the outcome. Limited numbers of qualitatively superior Tiger IIs could simply not stem the flood of enemy armor.

THE IS-2

When the Red Army transitioned to the strategic offensive in early 1943 their skill in operational deception increasingly enabled them to mass against specific battlefield sectors, often without the Germans realizing the degree to which they were outnumbered until it was too late. Purpose-built to help create a breach in the enemy's front-line defenses the IS-2's relatively light weight, thick armor, and powerful main gun made the design ideal for such hazardous tip-of-the-spear operations. Once a gap was created, follow-up armored and mechanized formations were freed to initiate the exploitation and pursuit phase of the Red Army's "deep battle" doctrine. Here, more nimble vehicles such as the T-34 could concentrate on moving into an enemy's flank and rear areas to attack their logistics and command and control capabilities. Unlike the mechanically unreliable KV-1, the IS-2 had a surprisingly high life expectancy of some 1,100km. Able to cover considerable distances on its own, as evidenced during the Vistula–Oder Offensive, it remained at the fore of Soviet offensive operations until the end of the war.

With some 20 HE rounds out of an ammunition complement of 28, the IS-2 was well suited to attacking targets such as fortifications, buildings, personnel, and transport vehicles. In this capacity its heavy, two-piece ammunition and slow loading and reaction times were not much of an issue. Against armor such delays could prove catastrophic. Should the 122mm D-25T gun score a hit, however, its relatively low-velocity projectiles imparted considerable force that could severely damage what they could not penetrate. Having a large quantity of low-grade propellant, its rounds created a considerable amount of smoke that could reveal its firing position. Its periscope did not provide all-around viewing or quick targeting reconciliation, and traversing the large, overhanging barrel was often impeded when the vehicle was not on level terrain. Thoughts of increasing the mantlet thickness were stillborn as any additional weight to the turret's front would only exacerbate the problem. In a potentially fast-paced tank battle, where being first to get a round on the target generally decided the contest, the IS-2 was often at a disadvantage.

As the IS-2's glacis presented a fairly small surface area its turret was the most likely target for enemy antitank weapons. As a defense against German handheld antitank weapons such as the *Panzerfaust* and *Panzerschreck*, IS-2 crews made increasing use of ad hoc metal turret screens or skirts to

A view of a Tiger II cupola showing the rough aiming device, which could be aligned with a small vertical rod (out of sight on the right) to allow the commander to provide a rough target direction to the gunner. A "Pilz" and armored plate for the ventilator fan are also shown. (Author's collection)

An IS-2 from 7th Guards Heavy Tank Brigade with quickly applied identification-friend-or-foe white turret stripe (the roof would have had a white cross) before the Brandenburg Gate, Berlin. As the unit had recently fought near the Arctic Circle the turret carries a white polar bear over a red star. The truck towing an antitank gun appears to be a Soviet ZIL-157. (DML)

disrupt the effect of the warhead's shaped-charge. Although prone to deformation in cramped urban environments, any such protection was better than nothing.

Although Soviet tank crews received less training than their German counterparts, especially for drivers, the IS-2's rugged construction was more forgiving than its Tiger II rival. Crew safety and comfort were secondary considerations to Soviet tank designers throughout the war, as evidenced by the rough application of welding and seaming, and construction techniques. Like the mass-produced T-34, the IS-2 was a relatively simple, rugged design that facilitated construction and in turn provided numbers to overwhelm the enemy and help bridge the gap between Soviet and German capabilities after a long period of German technology superiority.

During the fighting around Arnswalde IS-2s possessed better mobility, but the relatively open terrain and limited foliage plus the greater range of the Tiger II largely prohibited the Soviet tanks from getting close to the town – and the Germans focused on enemy tanks over other targets.

Throughout World War II the difficulty in developing, fielding, and supporting a variety of armored vehicle sizes and types was readily apparent. Manufacturing capability, raw material availability, design scope creep, and a pressing need for battlefield supremacy were only a few of the culprits. The resulting mix of light, medium, and heavy tanks and self-propelled guns, often with overlapping and redundant capabilities, and incompatible parts, was cost-prohibitive to maintain. Nations increasingly focused on a single main battle tank design (as well as light air-mobile varieties) that could be modified and upgraded as needed. As the 30-tonne American M4 Sherman and Soviet T-34 designs had proved themselves in combat, had been mass-produced, and were capable of accepting a variety of modifications, such logic continued into the postwar period. With the proliferation of portable, handheld antitank weapons many postulated armor's demise on the modern battlefield. Although the basic composition of tanks has changed little over 60 years, advancements in armor, armament, and performance, as well as communications and targeting, have allowed such vehicles to remain viable not just in high – but also in increasingly low-intensity combat environments.

THE AFTERMATH

With Germany having been at war for over five years, and only having steadily transitioned to a wartime economy after Albert Speer was made Minister of Armaments and War Production in 1942, battlefield attrition could not be maintained against the combined might of the Allied nations. Even with a significant rise in armored vehicle, aircraft, and ammunition production during 1944, by February of the following year Germany no longer possessed the materiel, manpower, or opportunity to launch anything save tactical counterattacks with limited objectives. Operation *Bagration*, the massive Soviet offensive that had shattered Army Group Center the previous summer, and the more recent Ardennes Offensive, had all but destroyed Germany's strategic reserves on the Eastern and Western Fronts respectively. Lacking such resources, even holding the invading enemy armies at Germany's Rhine and Oder river borders was by now a hopeless endeavor that no amount of propaganda could change.

Recent German offensives at Arnswalde, Colmar (Alsace-Lorraine), and Budapest illustrated that even the most determined German efforts did not exist in a vacuum, and that deficiencies in logistics, and a lack of air superiority and reinforcements, could not be corrected by will alone. Caught between their duty as German soldiers tasked with defending their homeland, and their mandatory oath to the person of Hitler, the Wehrmacht determined to fight to the end, if only to keep the Red Army from overrunning as much of Eastern Europe as possible, and to extract the multitudes of civilians trying to reach the safety of the West.

The idea of rigidly holding territory through the use of "fortresses" to siphon enemy forces from their spearheads and hamper their overall progress was a tactical expedient that achieved short-term benefits at best. Much as Stalin had done during *Barbarossa* in 1941, Hitler's "hold fast" mentality had hindered his commanders' ability to fight effectively once German military fortunes began to wane, following the Moscow campaign later that year. By his refusal to leave battlefield control to the experts on the spot, large numbers of German defenders became casualties while defending static and increasingly urbanized positions. Numerous "fortresses" throughout Pomerania, Silesia, and elsewhere eventually fell to Soviet forces, with the successful German relief of the Arnswalde garrison being something of an exception. For the Germans, their severe manpower, fuel, and ammunition shortages, and failing command-and-control infrastructure, meant that fortress defenders had negligible support and scant opportunity to be removed from such an environment either through their own, or by outside friendly efforts.

By the end of February 1945 US, British, and Commonwealth forces were preparing to move beyond the Roer and Rhine rivers and into central Germany. In the east Soviet forces were similarly making final adjustments prior to their final offensive to win the war in Europe. Once Zhukov reoriented his focus toward clearing the remainder of Pomerania further German offensive efforts south of the Ihna River were senseless. Fuel and ammunition were nearly gone and Himmler, never possessing the drive and skills required of a military commander, did little to actively adjust to the defensive save issuing an order to "regroup." Lacking adequate overall guidance, German resistance was sporadic and many vehicles had to be abandoned or disabled by their crews, with III (Germanic) SS Panzer Corps being forced to bear the brunt of Zhukov's renewed offensive.

Within two weeks of relieving the Arnswalde garrison, 1st and 2nd Belorussian Fronts pushed ahead into western and eastern Pomerania respectively. On March 4, Zhukov captured Stargard and established a bridgehead near Stettin, and on the following day he reached the Baltic Sea to effectively cut off the German Second Army to the east. Over the next few days the Soviets expanded their Baltic corridor to clear the Oder's east bank, and compress the Germans back on Danzig. Eleventh SS Panzer Army was subsequently split up, and its subordinate formations were reallocated to the defense of Berlin.

Although *Sonnenwende* failed to recapture Landsberg and cut off and destroy Red Army spearheads along the Oder River, the operation did reinforce Stalin's fears of German forces remaining along his Pomeranian flank. Instead of continuing to Berlin in early February, the Stavka postponed the operation until Zhukov and Rokossovsky had built up sufficient offensive forces and secured the Baltic coast. When Berlin was captured in May and the war in Europe ended, Soviet and Polish authorities forcibly expelled the remaining German residents of Pomerania, Silesia, and East Prussia. As the Soviet Union retained the territory it had taken from Poland in 1939, the Poles were in turn allowed to take these areas that had been German since the Middle Ages as part of the "Recovered Territories," which were then repopulated by Poles, Lithuanians, Belorussians, and Ukrainians.

BIBLIOGRAPHY

PRIMARY SOURCES

Note: "NII" refers to the Scientific Research Institute and "BIOS" to the British Intelligence Objectives Sub-Committee.

Briggs, Charles W. et al. *The Development and Manufacture of the Types of Cast Armor Employed by the US Army during WWII.* Ordnance Corps, 1942.

Hoffschmidt, E.J. and Tantum IV, W.H., eds. *Tank Data* (Aberdeen Proving Grounds Series). WE Inc., 1969.

NII (Research Lab)-48, Sverdlovsk. *Report of the Artillery Tests of the Armor Protection of IS-85 and IS-122.* 1944.

NII (Research Lab)-48, Sverdlovsk. *A Short Technical Report About Improving the IS-2's Armor.* 1944.

NII (Research Lab)-48, Sverdlovsk. *Studying the IS Tanks Being Destroyed in Summer–Autumn 1944.* 1945.

OKH. Merkblatt 47a/29 (Anhang 2 zur H. Dv. 1 a Seite 47a lfd. Nr. 29 und 30) – Merkblatt für Ausbildung und Einsatz der schweren Panzerkompanie Tiger. 1943.

People's Commissariat for Defense. *Combat Regulations for Tank and Mechanized Forces of the Red Army.* Parts I (Platoon and Company) and II (Battalion, Regiment, Brigade). 1944.

People's Commissariat for Defense. *Heavy Tank Manual.* 1944.

People's Commissariat of Heavy Industry. *Heavy Tanks and SP Guns in Action.* 1945.

Reed, E.L. and Kruegel, S.L. *A Study of the Mechanism of Penetration of Homogeneous Armor Plate*. Watertown Arsenal Laboratory, 1937.

SECONDARY SOURCES (BOOKS)

Babadzhanian, Hamazasp. *Tanks and Tank Forces*. Voenizdat, 1970.

Baryatinskiy, Mikhail. *The IS Tanks (IS-1, IS-2, IS-3)*. Ian Allan Publishing, 2006.

Bean, Tim and Fowler, Will. *Russian Tanks of World War II: Stalin's Armored Might*. Zenith Press, 2002.

BIOS. *German Steel Armour Piercing Projectiles and Theory of Penetration*. Final Report #1343, 1945.

BIOS. *German Tank Armour*. Final Report #653, 1946.

Bird, Lorrin R. and Livingston, Robert. *World War II Ballistics: Armor and Gunnery*. Overmatch Press, 2001.

Hahn, Fritz. *Waffen und Geheimwaffen des deutschen Heeres 1933–1943 Band 1 & Band 2*. Bernard & Graefe Verlag, 1987.

Harmon, Mark, ed. *Guns and Rubles: The Defense Industry in the Stalinist State*. Yale University Press, 2008.

Hohensee, Anneliese. *As Arnswalde Burned: A Documentation*. Self-published, 1968.

Jentz, Thomas. *Panzertruppen 2: The Complete Guide to the Creation and Combat Employment of Germany's Tank Force, 1943–1945*. Schiffer Publishing, Ltd., 1996.

Kurochkin, P.A., ed. *The Combined Arms Army in the Offensive*. Voenizdat, 1966.

Losik, O.A. *The Formation and Use of Soviet Tank Forces in the Years of the Great Patriotic War*. Voenizdat, 1979.

Ministry of Defense. *Order of Battle of the Soviet Army*. Part V (January–September 1945). Soviet General Staff Archives, 1990.

Mörke, Fritz. *Der Kampf um den Kreis Arnswalde im Jahre 1945*. Ostbrandenburgischen Kirchengemeinden, 1973.

Ogorkiewicz, Richard M. *Design and Development of Fighting Vehicles*. Macdonald, 1968.

Pavlov, A.G., Pavlov, Mikhail V., and Zheltov, Igor G. *20th Century Russian Armor*. Vol. 2, 1941–1945. Exprint, 2005.

Reinoss, Herbert. *Letzte Tage in Ostpreußen*. Langen/Müller, 2002.

Svirin, Mikhail. *Heavy IS Tanks*. Exprint, 2003.

Tieke, Wilhelm. *Tragedy of the Faithful: A History of the III. (germanisches) SS-Panzer-Korps*. J.J. Fedorowicz Publishing, Inc., 2001.

US War Dept. *Handbook on German Military Forces*. TM-E 30-451, March 1945.

US War Dept. *Handbook on U.S.S.R. Military Forces*. TM-E 30-430, November 1945.

INDEX

References to illustrations are shown in **bold**.